GCSE English

An Inspector Calls

by J.B. Priestley

You don't need to be a super-sleuth to write top essays about *An Inspector Calls*, but this brilliant CGP Workbook is well worth investigating...

It's bursting with questions to test you on the play's plot, characters, context, themes and the writer's techniques — plus plenty of realistic exam practice to build up the skills you'll need to do well on the day.

So don't crack under cross-examination in your GCSEs — get your story straight with CGP!

The Workbook

CONTENTS

CONTENTS

Section Four — The Writer's Techniques

Section Five — Exam Buster

Published by CGP

Editors:
Lucy Forsyth
Louise McEvoy
Rebecca Tate

Contributor:
John Sanders

With thanks to Emma Crighton and Nicola Woodfin for the proofreading.
With thanks to Jan Greenway for the copyright research.

Acknowledgements:

Cover photograph by Owen Howells with kind permission of The Torch Theatre, Milford Haven.

With thanks to Vishal Sharma & Altrincham Garrick Playhouse for permission to use the images on pages 1, 16, 20 and 31.

With thanks to Arenapal for permission to use the images on pages 3, 5, 6, 18 and 37.

With thanks to Rex Features for permission to use the images on pages 9, 17 and 27.

With thanks to Keith Pattison & Theatre by the Lake for permission to use the images on pages 10, 14, 25 and 29.

With thanks to Simon Gough Photography for permission to use the images on pages 19 and 38.

ISBN: 978 1 78294 776 9

Printed by Elanders Ltd, Newcastle upon Tyne.

Clipart from Corel®

How to Use this Book

Practise the four main skills you'll need for the exam

Each question tests <u>one or more</u> of the <u>four skills</u> you'll be tested on in the <u>exam</u>. You'll need to:

1) Write about the text in a <u>thoughtful way</u>, <u>picking out</u> appropriate <u>examples</u> and <u>quotations</u> to back up your opinions.

2) <u>Identify</u> and <u>explain</u> features of the play's <u>form</u>, <u>structure</u> and <u>language</u>. Using <u>subject terminology</u>, show how the author uses these to create <u>characters</u> and <u>settings</u>, explore <u>themes</u> and affect the <u>audience's reactions</u>.

3) Write about the play's <u>context</u> in your exam.

4) Write in a <u>clear</u>, <u>well-structured</u> and <u>accurate</u> way. <u>5%</u> of the marks in your English Literature GCSE are for <u>spelling</u>, <u>punctuation</u> and <u>grammar</u>.

> Most exam boards will want you to write about context. Ask your teacher if you're not sure.

You can use this workbook with the CGP Text Guide

1) This book is perfect to use with CGP's <u>Text Guide</u> for *An Inspector Calls*. It matches <u>each section</u> of the Text Guide, so you can test your knowledge <u>bit by bit</u>.

2) The workbook covers all the <u>important</u> parts of the text that you'll need to know about for the exam — <u>plot</u>, <u>characters</u>, <u>context</u>, <u>themes</u> and the <u>writer's techniques</u>.

3) The questions refer to the text <u>in detail</u> — you'll need a <u>copy</u> of the play to make the most of the workbook.

©Vishal Sharma/Altrincham Garrick Playhouse

It prepares you for the exam every step of the way

1) The exam section is jam-packed with <u>useful advice</u>. It <u>guides</u> you through how to tackle the exam, from understanding the questions to building great answers. There's also an easy-to-read <u>mark scheme</u>, which you can use to mark <u>sample answers</u> and improve answers of your <u>own</u>.

2) There are four pages of <u>practice exam questions</u> spread across the book. They give you the opportunity to use what you've revised in each section to write a <u>realistic answer</u>.

3) <u>Exam tips</u> and extra <u>practice exam questions</u> are included throughout the book. There are also helpful <u>revision tasks</u> designed to get you thinking more creatively. These are marked with <u>stamps</u>.

4) You can find <u>answers</u> to all of the <u>questions</u> and <u>tasks</u> at the back of the book.

5) Each section contains at least one '<u>Skills Focus</u>' page. These pages help you to practise important skills <u>individually</u>. You can tackle them in <u>any order</u> and prioritise the skills you find the <u>hardest</u>.

I'm sure you have a Birling desire to find out more...

Now you've got to grips with the essentials of how to use this book, you're ready to enter the big wide world of workbook questions. All you need is a pen, a copy of the play and a snack of choice for the road... mmm...

Section One — Analysis of Acts

Act One

Q1 Read from the beginning of the play until Mrs Birling says, **"Now stop it, you two."**
Decide whether each statement is **true** or **false**, and find a short quote to support your answer.

    a) Arthur Birling is keen to impress Gerald.   True: ☐   False: ☐

    Quote: ....

    b) Sheila is suspicious of Gerald's past behaviour.   True: ☐   False: ☐

    Quote: ....

    c) Eric feels completely relaxed around his family.   True: ☐   False: ☐

    Quote: ....

Q2 Find a quote to back up each of these statements.

    a) Arthur thinks that Sheila and Gerald's marriage will be good for his business.

    ....

    ....

    b) Sybil treats Sheila like a child.

    ....

Q3 What do we find out about Gerald's mother when Arthur talks to him **"in strict confidence"**?

    ....

    ....

Q4 What does Mr Birling say just before the Inspector rings the doorbell?
Explain why you think Priestley chose this point for the Inspector to arrive.

    Quote: ....

    ....

    Explanation: ....

    ....

    ....

The investigation starts

Q1 Put these events in order by numbering the boxes.
The first one has been done for you.

Inspector Goole announces that a girl has killed herself. ☐

Sheila tells the others what happened at Milwards. ☐

The Inspector shows a photograph to Mr Birling. ☐

Mr Birling and Gerald joke together. 1

The audience learns that Mr Birling sacked Eva Smith. ☐

Sheila is distressed when she hears about the girl's death. ☐

Q2 Why does Arthur think he isn't responsible for Eva's death?
Use a quote to back up your answer.

....

....

....

....

Q3 Briefly describe what you can tell about the relationship between Mr Birling and Eric in Act One.

....

....

Q4 Answer each question and then choose a quote from the text that supports your answer.

a) How does Mr Birling behave towards the Inspector when he is being questioned?

....

Quote: ....

b) What does Gerald think about Mr Birling's decision to sack Eva?

....

Quote: ....

c) How does Sheila feel about her own behaviour towards Eva?

....

Quote: ....

Section One — Analysis of Acts

Gerald becomes involved

Q1 How does Gerald's behaviour change once he has heard the name 'Daisy Renton'?

....

....

Q2 Read from "**Well, Gerald?**" to the end of Act One. How has Sheila's behaviour towards Gerald changed since the start of the play? Support your answer with quotes.

....

....

....

....

Q3 Looking at the same section as in Q2, find a quote to back up each of these statements.

a) Sheila is determined to find out the truth about Gerald's involvement with Eva/Daisy.

....

b) Gerald doesn't want to accept responsibility for Eva/Daisy's death.

....

c) Sheila knows that the Inspector is in control of the situation.

....

Q4 How does Priestley end Act One? Why do you think he does this?

....

....

....

....

At my next party, I think I'll have a magician instead...

Write a paragraph that describes how the Birlings are shown to be a 'happy family' at the start of the play. Then explain how the audience's view of the family has changed by the end of Act One.

Section One — Analysis of Acts

Act Two

Gerald's lies are uncovered

Q1 In your own words, explain why Sheila stays after the Inspector has finished questioning her.

....

....

....

....

Q2 Find a quote which shows that Sheila feels uneasy when her mother first speaks to the Inspector.

....

Q3 Put these events in order by numbering the boxes.
The first one has been done for you.

Eva/Daisy became Gerald's mistress. ☐

Eva Smith lost her job at Milwards and changed her name. 1

Gerald found accommodation for Eva/Daisy. ☐

Eva/Daisy went to the seaside to reflect on what had happened. ☐

Gerald ended the affair. ☐

Gerald met Eva/Daisy in the bar at the Palace Variety Theatre. ☐

© Marilyn Kingwill/ArenaPAL

Q4 What explanation does Sheila give for postponing her engagement to Gerald?

....

....

Q5 Complete the passage below.

When the Inspector starts questioning Gerald about Daisy Renton, Sheila is ....

to find out more details. She talks to Gerald in a .... way but is glad that

he is being .... Mrs Birling thinks that Gerald's affair is ....

However, Mr Birling suggests that it was .... for young men to have affairs.

Sybil won't accept responsibility

Q1 Put these events in order by numbering the boxes.
The first one has been done for you.

Mrs Birling claims not to recognise the photo the Inspector shows her. ☐

The front door slams — Eric has left. ☐

Sheila accuses her mother of not telling the truth. ☐

The Inspector starts to question Mrs Birling about her charity work. ☐

The audience finds out that Mrs Birling has recently seen Eva/Daisy. ☐

Gerald leaves the house. 1

Q2 Why was Sybil Birling "**prejudiced**" against Eva/Daisy's case?
Give two reasons and use quotes to support your answer.

....

....

....

....

Q3 Sybil admits that she used her "**influence**" to make sure her charity refused
Eva/Daisy's request for help. What does this tell the audience about Sybil?

....

....

....

Q4 Find a quote from Act Two to back up each of these statements.

a) Sybil does not regret her actions towards Eva/Daisy.

....

....

b) The Inspector thinks that Sybil should accept responsibility.

....

....

© Pete Jones/ArenaPAL

Section One — Analysis of Acts

The Inspector catches Sybil out

Q1 Read from where Sheila says **"Thank goodness for that!"** to where Sybil says **"Oh, stop it, both of you."** Decide whether each statement is **true** or **false**, and find a quote to support your answer.

a) The committee was Eva/Daisy's last resort. **True:** ☐ **False:** ☐

Quote: ....

b) Sheila agrees with her mother's actions. **True:** ☐ **False:** ☐

Quote: ....

c) Sybil's actions could lead to unwanted publicity for the Birlings. **True:** ☐ **False:** ☐

Quote: ....

Q2 The Inspector sets a trap for Sybil. In your own words, explain how he does this.

....

....

....

Q3 Why did Eva/Daisy refuse to take money from Eric?

....

Q4 Answer each question, choosing a quote from the text that supports your answer.

a) What does Sybil think should happen to the father of Eva/Daisy's child?

....

Quote: ....

b) How does Sheila feel as she listens to her mother talking about the father of Eva/Daisy's child?

....

Quote: ....

This really is the mother of all mix-ups...

Look back at Acts One and Two. Choose a key event in each act and write a short paragraph about its significance. Explain what happens, who is involved and what the immediate consequences are.

 ☐   ☐   ☐

Section One — Analysis of Acts

Act Three

It's Eric's turn to be questioned

Q1 Think about the atmosphere on stage at the very end of Act Two and the very beginning of Act Three. How does Priestley create tension here?

....

....

....

....

Q2 Identify who said each of these phrases and explain what it suggests about how they're feeling.

a) "But I didn't know it was *you* — I never dreamt."   Said by: ....

Shows that: ....

b) "Don't start on that. I want to get on."   Said by: ....

Shows that: ....

Q3 How did Eric react to Eva/Daisy's pregnancy? Use quotes to support your answer.

....

....

....

Q4 Read from where Mrs Birling says "**Eric! You stole money?**" to where Eric says "**My God — I'm not likely to forget.**" Find a quote to back up each of the following statements.

a) Eric didn't feel that he could rely on his father for help.

....

b) Eric blames his mother for the death of his and Eva/Daisy's child.

....

c) Eric feels that he has been neglected by his mother.

....

The Inspector gives his verdict

Q1 For each of the quotes below, write the name of the character the Inspector is talking to.

   a) "**You turned her away when she most needed help.**"

   Said to: ....

   b) "**Just used her... as if she was an animal...**"

   Said to: ....

   c) "**You started it.**"

   Said to: ....

© Alastair Muir/REX/Shutterstock

Q2 Read the Inspector's speech from "**But just remember this.**" to "**Good night.**"
Summarise the key message that the Inspector is trying to get across.

....

....

....

Q3 Read from where Mr Birling says "**You're the one I blame for this.**" to where he says
"**Nothing much has happened!**" Find a quote to back up each of the following statements.

   a) Mr Birling is worried about his reputation.

   ....

   b) Sheila accepts responsibility for her actions.

   ....

   c) Eric thinks his father's concerns are petty.

   ....

Q4 Whose reaction to the Inspector's verdict do you agree with the most? Why?

....

....

....

Section One — Analysis of Acts

The Birlings can't agree

Q1   Complete the passage below with the correct characters. You'll need some names more than once.

The Birling family is divided when the Inspector leaves. .... is the first to

suggest that .... might have been a fake. .... says this makes

"all the difference", but .... and .... disagree with him.

.... is cross with .... and .... for not

"standing up" to ...., and for being tricked into discussing their **"private affairs"**.

Q2   What do the Birlings discuss in Act Three after the Inspector has left? Tick the correct boxes.

If Eric will join the family business ☐

Whether there really was a suicide that day ☐

If the Inspector was a real police inspector ☐

The date for Sheila and Gerald's wedding ☐

How much the Inspector knew in advance ☐

Q3   What does Gerald find out while he is out of the house?

....

Q4   How do Mr Birling and Eric react differently to the idea that Eva/Daisy was several different girls?

....

....

....

Q5   The characters respond differently to the news that no girl has died in the infirmary that day. Identify who says each of these sentences and explain what it shows about how that character is feeling.

a) "The whole story's just a lot of moonshine."   Said by: ....

Shows that: ....

b) "But you're forgetting one thing I still can't forget."   Said by: ....

Shows that: ....

The play ends with a twist

Q1 Read from where Mr Birling says, "**Going to bed, young woman?**" to where Sheila says, "**I must think.**" Decide whether each statement is **true** or **false**, and find a quote to support your answer.

a) Mr and Mrs Birling's behaviour makes Sheila feel uncomfortable.　**True:** ☐　**False:** ☐

Quote: ....

b) Gerald believes that he and Sheila can move on and forget.　**True:** ☐　**False:** ☐

Quote: ....

c) The older generation doesn't take the events of the play seriously.　**True:** ☐　**False:** ☐

Quote: ....

Q2 What happens at the end of the play to remind the audience of the beginning?

....

....

Q3 How do you think the characters will act when the new police inspector arrives? Back up your answer with reference to the text.

....

....

....

Q4 Do you think the Birling family will be punished for their actions? Explain your answer.

....

....

....

....

My verdict? The play's all right, but I prefer musicals...

Thinking about the play as a whole, write a summary of the Birlings' and Gerald's involvement in Eva/Daisy's death. Your summary should include:

- a sentence or two explaining how each character was involved with Eva/Daisy
- a short paragraph stating who was the most responsible for her death, and why.

 ☐　 ☐　 ☐

Section One — Analysis of Acts

Using Quotes

In the exam, you'll need to use quotes from the play to back up your argument. It's worth practising this skill because your answer will be much more convincing if you can give evidence for your views. You won't have the text with you in the exam, so you'll have to learn some important quotes off by heart. This page gives you chance to think about how to choose good quotes and use them well — have a go at the questions below and you'll soon be well on your way to exam success.

Q1 Fill in the text about how to use quotes in your answers.

A good quote is .... — you should write your quote exactly as it appears in the text. Good quotes are also highly .... to the point being made, so don't choose something off topic. A bad quote will be ...., and won't support the point you're discussing. A good quote will be .... in the sentence, rather than just added on afterwards. Only use the most .... part of a sentence or passage — it's easier to remember short quotes. Also, a quote shouldn't just .... your point. It should give new information.

Q2 Look at these examples and decide which use quotes well and which use them badly.

> a) The Inspector displays sympathy for Eva/Daisy. He tells the Birlings that she enjoyed "being among pretty clothes" and asks them to put themselves in her position.
>
> b) Mr Birling is pleased about Sheila and Gerald's engagement because he thinks he'll be able to work with Gerald's father to achieve "lower costs and higher prices".
>
> c) Eric believes that his mother "never even tried" to understand.
>
> d) Mrs Birling believes that the baby's father is completely responsible — she says that he is "entirely responsible".
>
> e) In Act Three, Eric refuses to just move on like his parents, telling them, "I still feel the same about it, and that's why I don't feel like sitting down and having a nice cosy talk."

Good quote usage: ....   Bad quote usage: ....

Q3 Choose one of the examples you identified as bad in Q2 and improve it.

....

....

....

P.E.E.D.

To get a great mark, you have to do more than just comment on the text — your answer needs to be well-structured and developed. The P.E.E.D. method is a brilliant way to make sure you do this.

For each **point** you make in your answer, provide a supporting quote or a specific **example**, then **explain** how it backs up your point. Finally, **develop** your point by explaining the effect it has on the audience, or making a link with another part of the play, a different theme or the play's context.

Q1 None of the sample answers below have used P.E.E.D. correctly. For each, say which stage of P.E.E.D. is missing, then write a sentence you could include to improve the answer.

a)

> The Inspector uses shock tactics to challenge the Birlings. He frequently uses emotive language to describe what happened to Eva/Daisy, for example saying that the disinfectant "Burnt her inside out." The audience realises that he is on her side and wants the Birlings to see the error of their ways.

Missing stage: .... Addition: ....

....

....

b)

> Sheila becomes more assertive as the play progresses. This demonstrates that she is able to think for herself. This is also shown at the end of the play when she opposes the views of her parents — she believes that even if a girl didn't die, they all still behaved immorally and need to be more responsible in future.

Missing stage: .... Addition: ....

....

....

c)

> Mrs Birling displays class prejudice when she talks about Eva/Daisy, proclaiming that it was "simply absurd" for a girl of her class to be concerned about morality. Mrs Birling believes that members of the working class are inferior and have lower moral standards than the middle and upper classes.

Missing stage: .... Addition: ....

....

....

Section One — Analysis of Acts

Section Two — Characters

The Inspector

Q1 Look at the stage directions that introduce the Inspector, starting with *"The Inspector need not be a big man..."* What does this description suggest about the Inspector?

....

....

....

Q2 Find a quote from the play that shows that the Inspector is:

a) powerful

Quote: ....

b) mysterious

Quote: ....

c) outspoken

Quote: ....

Q3 Briefly summarise what the Inspector believes about society.

....

....

....

....

© Keith Pattison/Theatre by the Lake

Q4 Look at these statements about the role of the Inspector in the play. Decide which ones are **true** and which ones are **false**.

	True	False
The Inspector highlights the immorality of the Birling family.	☐	☐
The Inspector makes the audience feel sorry for the middle class.	☐	☐
The Inspector often provides comic relief in the play.	☐	☐
The Inspector puts across Priestley's opinions to the audience.	☐	☐
The Inspector controls the pace of the action in the play.	☐	☐

Q5 The Inspector often gives orders to Gerald and the Birlings.
What does this make the audience think about the Inspector?

....

....

....

Q6 Think about the way the Inspector questions Gerald and the Birlings.
How does his style of questioning force them to confess their roles in Eva/Daisy's death?

....

....

....

Q7 Give two examples from the play where the Inspector behaves
in a way that goes against the social rules of the time.

1) ....

2) ....

Q8 The Inspector's surname is Goole. Why do you think Priestley chose this name?

....

....

Q9 Do you think it matters if the Inspector isn't a real police inspector?

....

....

....

....

 ☐   ☐   ☐

Section Two — Characters

Arthur Birling

Q1 Think of three adjectives to describe Arthur Birling's personality, then find a quote to back up each one.

Adjectives: ....

Quote 1: ....

Quote 2: ....

Quote 3: ....

Q2 Fill in the gaps in the table below. The first one has been done for you.

Feature of the play	What it reveals about Mr Birling
a) Mr Birling is worried that the Inspector's findings will cause a public scandal.	His reputation is important to him.
b) Mr Birling has more long speeches than the other characters.	
c) Mr Birling tries to intimidate the Inspector when the Inspector questions him.	
d) Mr Birling doesn't think there will be a war.	

Q3 How responsible do you think Mr Birling is for Eva/Daisy's death? Explain your answer.

....

....

Q4 How does Mr Birling react in Act Three when he thinks the Inspector's visit was a hoax? What does this show about whether his views have changed during the play?

....

....

....

I take you, Arthur Birling, in richness and in wealth...

Imagine you're Arthur Birling. Write a job advert for a new factory worker at Birling and Company. Include the qualities you look for in a good worker and list any qualities that you think are unsuitable.

Section Two — Characters

Sybil Birling

Q1 Write a short summary of the role that Mrs Birling played in Eva/Daisy's death.

....

....

....

Q2 Why do you think being respected and upholding
traditional values is so important to Mrs Birling?

....

....

....

© Jane Hobson/REX/Shutterstock

Q3 Give one way that Mrs Birling's prejudices influence her treatment of Eva/Daisy.

....

....

Q4 Mrs Birling thinks the Inspector has a lower social status than her. How is this
reflected in the way she treats the Inspector? Find a quote to back up your answer.

....

....

Quote: ....

Q5 Priestley describes Mrs Birling as a "***rather cold woman***" in the stage directions at the
beginning of the play. Do you agree with this description? Give reasons for your answer.

....

....

....

I certainly wouldn't want to live in a 'Sybilised' society...

Sybil's actions and attitudes are shaped by the society she lives in. To understand her character fully,
you'll need to think about the context of the play, including when it was written and set (see p.24).

Sheila Birling

Q1 Fill in the gaps in the passage below.

© Francis Loney/ArenaPAL

Priestley presents Sheila as .... and perceptive. She suspects that Gerald has been keeping a .... from her and guesses the truth about his .... before he admits it. Sheila is also the quickest to understand that .... is more than he seems, and is the first in her family to realise that .... got Eva/Daisy pregnant.

Q2 Find a quote where Sheila uses emotive language to talk about Eva/Daisy. What does the emotive language in the quote show about how Sheila is feeling?

Quote: ....

Explanation: ....

....

Q3 Explain how Sheila's character changes as a result of the Inspector's visit.

....

....

....

....

Q4 At the end of the play, Sheila postpones her engagement to Gerald. Do you think this was a difficult decision for Sheila to make? Explain your answer.

....

....

....

PRACTICE TASK

Sheila's bright — maybe that's why she sees the light...

Write a letter from Sheila to her parents, persuading them to take responsibility for their part in Eva/Daisy's death. Use what Sheila learns during the play to explain why they should change their attitudes.

Section Two — Characters

Eric Birling

Q1 In Act One, Eric laughs unexpectedly at dinner and is described as being *"not quite at ease"*. Why do you think Priestley makes him behave in this way at the start of the play?

....

....

Q2 Find short quotes to back up the following statements.

a) Eric has a difficult relationship with his parents.

Quote: ....

b) Eric didn't care deeply for Eva/Daisy.

Quote: ....

Q3 How is Eric's reaction to the idea that the Inspector is a hoax different to Mr and Mrs Birling's?

....

....

Q4 Who do you think mistreated Eva/Daisy the most — Eric or Gerald? Explain your answer.

© Simon Gough Photography

....

....

....

....

Q5 'The play suggests that the way Eric treated Eva/Daisy was unusual for a man with a respectable social status at that time.' Explain whether you agree or disagree with this statement.

....

....

....

PRACTICE TASK

Eric's worst card game? Definitely 'Happy Families'...

Think about how Eric treated Eva/Daisy and how he feels about it by the end of the play. Do you think Priestley wants the audience to forgive Eric? Write a couple of paragraphs to explain your answer.

Section Two — Characters

Gerald Croft

Q1 Priestley shows both good and bad sides to Gerald's personality.
Find an example of each and give a quote to support your answer.

Good: ....

Quote: ....

Bad: ....

Quote: ....

Q2 Explain why Gerald's background and social status are important to Mr Birling.

....

....

....

Q3 Find a quote where Gerald tries to challenge the Inspector's authority. Why does he do this?

Quote: ....

Explanation: ....

....

Q4 At the end of the play, Gerald doesn't seem to have learnt anything from
the Inspector's visit. How does Priestley show this to the audience?

....

....

....

....

© Vishal Sharma/Altrincham Garrick Playhouse

The "wonderful Fairy Prince" — what a nickname...

What is the significance of the relationship between Gerald and Sheila in *An Inspector Calls*?

You should write about:
- how Priestley presents their relationship
- how their relationship develops and why this is important in the play.

Section Two — Characters

Eva Smith / Daisy Renton

Q1 Write a short quote about Eva/Daisy said by each of the characters below.

Mr Birling: ....

Sheila: ....

Gerald: ....

Mrs Birling: ....

Eric: ....

Q2 Use the quotes you found in the question above to come up with four adjectives to describe Eva/Daisy.

1) .... 3) ....

2) .... 4) ....

Q3 The Inspector often uses emotive language to talk about Eva/Daisy, describing her as "**alone**", "**friendless**" and "**desperate**". Explain how this affects the audience's feelings towards Eva/Daisy.

....

Q4 How does Priestley restrict Eva/Daisy's presence in the play to show that she is powerless?

....

....

....

Q5 What is the character of Eva/Daisy a symbol for in the play? Explain your answer.

....

....

....

....

 Poor old Eva/Daisy — talk about an identity crisis...

PRACTICE TASK

All this Eva/Daisy stuff can get pretty confusing. Make a timeline of what happened to her, from when Mr Birling sacked her to her suicide. If the exact date of an event isn't clear, make an informed guess.

Making Links

A great way to develop your answer is to make links between the points you've made and other parts of the text. You could write about similar events, other times characters behave in the same way or other places where a theme is presented. This page focuses on making links between the characters' actions during the play, which will be a good recap of how and why the characters change or stay the same. Have a look back through the 'Characters' section if you need inspiration.

Q1 Fill in the table below with examples to illustrate the key points about each character. You can either use quotes or just explain what happens, as long as it's a precise example.

Character	Key Point	Example One	Example Two
Arthur	Arthur is obsessed with his social standing.		
Eva/Daisy	Eva/Daisy is powerless.		
Sheila	Sheila is not as naive as her parents think.		

Q2 Now do the same for the characters below. This time, you'll need to think of your own key point about them.

Character	Key Point	Example One	Example Two
Sybil			
Eric			
The Inspector			

Practice Questions

Here are some exam-style questions to get stuck into. There's quite a lot to be getting on with, so don't try to do them all at once. Find one you like the look of and jot down around five points you could write about. Then turn your plan into a full answer. Make sure you include an introduction and a conclusion.

Q1 Explore how Priestley presents the Inspector as a figure of authority in the play.

Q2 In what ways does Sheila change as the play progresses?

You should write about:
- how Priestley presents Sheila in the play
- how Sheila's attitude is changed by the Inspector's visit.

Q3 Explore how the character of Mrs Birling is used to present ideas about class in the play.

Q4 What does the relationship between Eric and Mr Birling tell the audience about each of them as characters?

You should write about:
- the nature of their relationship and its development over the course of the play
- what this shows about each of their characters.

Q5 **"It's what happened to the girl and what we all did to her that matters."** (Eric, Act Three)

Explain the importance of the character of Eva/Daisy in *An Inspector Calls*.

Section Three — Context and Themes

Britain in 1912 and 1945

Q1 Complete the passage below.

The play is set in 1912. At that time, there were .... divisions in

British society. There was a strong link between .... and power —

.... people had more power than .... people.

People in need often had to rely on .... Women's rights were quite

.... For example, women weren't allowed to ....,

and their families and .... had a lot of control over them.

Q2 Read Arthur Birling's speech in Act One from "**Just because
the Kaiser...**" to "**...in the Balkans.**" Why is he wrong?

....

....

Q3 Find a quote where Mr Birling makes another incorrect prediction. Explain why he is wrong.

Quote: ....

Wrong because: ....

Q4 Mr Birling tells Gerald and Sheila that they'll be marrying at "**a very good time**". Would an
audience in the mid-1940s have thought his optimism was justified? Explain your answer.

....

....

....

....

....

I reckon Mr Birling should give his crystal ball a wipe...

To get a good mark in the exam, you'll need to show you're aware of the play's context. Make sure
you know what the world was like in 1912, when it was set, and in 1945, when Priestley was writing.

Family Life

Q1 Read the statements about middle-class family life in 1912.
Decide whether each one is **true** or **false**.

<table>
<tr><td></td><td>True</td><td>False</td></tr>
<tr><td>Family members had clearly defined roles.</td><td>☐</td><td>☐</td></tr>
<tr><td>Children were expected to respect and obey their parents.</td><td>☐</td><td>☐</td></tr>
<tr><td>There were different rules for men and women.</td><td>☐</td><td>☐</td></tr>
<tr><td>Wealthy middle-class women did all of the housework.</td><td>☐</td><td>☐</td></tr>
</table>

Q2 'Birling family life is far from perfect.' Find three
short quotes from Act One to back up this statement.

Quote 1: ....

....

Quote 2: ....

....

Quote 3: ....

© Keith Pattison/Theatre by the Lake

Q3 What impact does the Inspector's questioning have on the hierarchy of the Birling family?

....

....

....

Q4 How do you think the relationships between the Birling
family members will change after the events of the play?

....

....

....

....

Think your family life is a strain? Well, it's all relative...

Write a couple of paragraphs about the family roles that Sheila and Mr Birling have. Include how far
they fulfil traditional family roles at the start of the play, and whether these have changed by the end.

Social Class

Q1   Fill in the table below to give information about the three classes presented in *An Inspector Calls*.

Class	Represented by...	Quote that shows this
Working class		
Middle class		
Upper class		

Q2   Sheila, Gerald and Mrs Birling all take advantage of their social position in their behaviour towards Eva/Daisy. Give an example of this for each character.

Sheila: ....

....

Gerald: ....

....

Mrs Birling: ....

....

Q3   In Act Two, Mrs Birling refers to Eva/Daisy as **"a girl of that sort."** What does this suggest about the attitude of the middle and upper classes to working-class people?

....

....

....

Q4   Read the following statements about Mr Birling.
Which one best describes his attitude to social class?

Mr Birling is satisfied with his social standing.   ☐

Mr Birling looks for ways to improve his position in society.   ☐

Mr Birling doesn't respect the higher classes.   ☐

Q5 How does Priestley use the character of Eric to give a negative impression of the middle class?

....

....

....

....

Q6 How do you think Priestley wants the audience to react to Mr Birling's dismissal of Eva Smith from her job in his works?

....

....

....

....

© Jane Hobson/REX/Shutterstock

Q7 Find an example of when the Inspector uses language that suggests that he sympathises with the working class.

....

....

....

....

Q8 How does Priestley use the character of Eva/Daisy to challenge Mr and Mrs Birling's attitude towards class?

....

....

....

....

My teacher thinks all classes should be working classes...

Imagine you are Sybil. Write a paragraph justifying your refusal to help Eva/Daisy — think about the influence of social class. Then, pretend to be Eva/Daisy and write a paragraph defending your actions.

Section Three — Context and Themes

Young and Old

Q1 Complete the sentences about the Birlings and Gerald below.

Arthur and Sybil Birling represent the .... generation. Their views are quite

.... and they think authority and social status should be ....·

The younger generation is represented by .... and ....·

They .... the beliefs of their parents and develop their own views.

Technically, Gerald belongs to the .... generation. However, he usually

agrees with .... and ....·

Q2 Answer each question, choosing a quote from the text that supports your answer.

a) What does Eric think about Mr Birling's treatment of Eva Smith?

....

Quote: ....

b) How does Eric react to Mr Birling's worry that he won't get a knighthood?

....

Quote: ....

c) What does Sheila think about her parents at the end of the play?

....

Quote: ....

Q3 Gerald is one of the younger characters but, unlike Eric and Sheila, he doesn't
change during the play. What message do you think Priestley wanted to get across?

....

....

....

I've got Arthur mind to dock your pocket money...

Make sure you can give examples of clashes between the generations. Think about how Eric and
Sheila challenge their parents' authority, and how this makes Arthur and Sybil feel threatened.

Section Three — Context and Themes

Men and Women

Q1 Complete the table to show three stereotypes of women presented in Act One.

© Keith Pattison/Theatre by the Lake

Stereotype	Quote that shows this

Q2 Sheila and Eva/Daisy challenge gender roles. Give examples of this in your own words.

Example 1: ....

Example 2: ....

Example 3: ....

Q3 How does the men's language change in Act Three after the women have left?

....

....

....

Q4 How has Mr Birling's position as the 'dominant male' changed by the end of the play?

....

....

....

....

Priestley's all about the girl power...

This theme links to the theme of social class — at the start of the 20th century, middle-class men, middle-class women and working-class women had to conform to very different social expectations.

Section Three — Context and Themes

Judgement

Q1 Priestley wants the audience to judge the Birlings' immoral behaviour. Find a quote to back up each of these statements.

    a) Mr Birling treats his workers harshly.

    ....

    ....

    b) Sheila's behaviour towards Eva Smith was a result of her own vanity.

    ....

    ....

Q2 How does Priestley create the impression that the Birlings are on trial?

....

....

....

Q3 In Act Three, Eric says **"He was our police inspector all right."** What does this show about Eric's understanding of judgement?

....

....

....

Q4 The Inspector leaves well before the end of the play. Why is this important for the theme of judgement?

....

....

....

Sorry really does seem to be the hardest word...

Make an essay plan for the following question:
How is the Inspector used to explore the theme of judgement in *An Inspector Calls*?

Learning about Life

Q1 Tick the statements that are **true**.

The Inspector shows how Mrs Birling is blinded by her prejudices. ☐

Mrs Birling remains unaffected by events throughout the play. ☐

At the end of Act Three, Mrs Birling regrets her actions. ☐

Mrs Birling tries to rewrite events to her own advantage. ☐

© Vishal Sharma/Altrincham Garrick Playhouse

Q2 In Act Three, Mr Birling claims, "**I've learnt plenty tonight.**"
Give one argument for and one argument against this statement.

....

....

....

Q3 Sheila arguably learns the most about how her actions can affect other people.
Find a quote from each act to show how her understanding grows.

Act One: ....

....

Act Two: ....

....

Act Three: ....

....

Q4 What does the Inspector teach the other characters about the lives of working-class people?

....

....

....

EXAM PRACTICE

Ignorance is bliss — until you get to the exam...

Explain how Priestley presents the theme of learning in *An Inspector Calls*.

You should write about:
- which characters learn and how Priestley presents their development
- why some of the characters don't learn.

Social Responsibility

Q1 Complete the table to show the characters' views about social responsibility.

Being socially responsible means being considerate to everyone in society.

Character	Beginning of play	End of play
Gerald		
	Doesn't think about how his behaviour affects others, acts immaturely.	
Sheila		

Q2 Find three things the Inspector says that show his views about social responsibility.

Quote 1: ....

Quote 2: ....

Quote 3: ....

Q3 When the Inspector questions Mrs Birling about her actions towards Eva/Daisy, she says **"I did nothing I'm ashamed of"**. What does this show about her sense of social responsibility?

....

....

....

....

Q4 Priestley gives Arthur Birling views about social responsibility that are the opposite of his own. Why has he done this?

....

....

....

Another party? OK — I accept my social responsibilities...

'Priestley's message about social responsibility is still relevant today.' Do you agree? Write a short paragraph arguing for or against this statement, using evidence from the text to back up your view.

Writing about Context

To get a high mark in the exam, you have to know about the play's context. *An Inspector Calls* was written in the 1940s but set in 1912, so you need to have an understanding of what society was like at those times, and which important historical events took place around then. Adding contextual information and linking it to the key themes in the play will help you improve your answer. The questions on this page will get you thinking about context and how to use it in your responses.

Q1 Read the sample answer extracts below and underline the contextual information.

a) Arthur Birling is determined to be seen as the strong, unquestioned head of the household, but his children challenge his position. In Act Three, Eric makes it clear that he thinks Arthur's concerns about his reputation are laughable in light of events and says that he is "ashamed" of both his parents. This challenges traditional ideas about family life, because at the start of the 20th century children were expected to respect their parents' authority. Families had a clear structure, with the father at the top of the hierarchy. Eric mocks his father, showing that he doesn't respect him and is thinking for himself. The fact that he is "ashamed" suggests that he believes he knows better than Arthur and can therefore judge his behaviour, which goes against the social expectation of the time.

b) Arthur Birling believes that his responsibility is to "keep labour costs down" rather than to promote the welfare of his workers. He employs hundreds of young women, who "keep changing". The casual way he refers to his workers losing and gaining employment suggests he cares little for their welfare and highlights the power he has over them as a middle-class businessman. At the time the play is set, there was a rigid class system and those in society with the most money had the most power. Sheila's objection that the workers "aren't cheap labour — they're *people*" reveals how Mr Birling is abusing his position of power and emphasises the unfairness of the class system to the audience.

Q2 Write down a piece of context that could be included in the sample answer below.

How does Priestley present ideas about gender in *An Inspector Calls*?

In *An Inspector Calls*, there is a lack of understanding between the male and female characters on certain issues. For example, Mrs Birling describes Gerald's affair with Daisy Renton as "disgusting", but Mr Birling implies that "a lot of young men" behave in this way.

....

....

....

....

Practice Questions

Priestley has rammed his play full of complex themes, so you need to make sure you've got your head around them all before your exam. The best way to do that is to practise, so we've got some more lovely questions for you to have a bash at. Plan your answers carefully and check through your work at the end.

Q1 How do tensions between the generations develop in *An Inspector Calls*?
You should write about:
- how the relationships between the characters change throughout the play
- the reasons for the divisions which appear.

Q2 Explain how Priestley challenges traditional gender roles in the play.

Q3 "**But these girls aren't cheap labour — they're *people*.**" (Sheila, Act One)

How does Priestley explore the relationship between morality and class?
Make sure you refer to the play's context when answering the question.

Q4 Explain how Priestley uses the Inspector to present the theme of social responsibility.
You should write about:
- how Priestley presents the Inspector in the play
- the messages conveyed by the Inspector.

Q5 Priestley wrote *An Inspector Calls* in 1945, but it is set in 1912.
In what ways is the play's context significant?

'An Inspector Calls' on the Stage

Q1 All of the action in the play takes place in the Birlings' dining room.
What atmosphere does Priestley create by only giving the play one setting?

....

Q2 Before the Inspector enters, the lighting is *"pink and intimate"*.

   a) Find the stage direction from the opening of the play that suggests how the lighting should
change when the Inspector arrives.

   Quote: ....

   b) Why do you think Priestley wanted the lighting to change in this way?

   ....

   ....

Q3 Look at the stage directions at the start of the play. Give two
ways that the set design shows the wealth of the Birling family.

   1) ....

   2) ....

Q4 The Inspector is dressed in a *"plain darkish suit"*, but the other characters on stage all wear
"evening dress of the period". Why do you think these characters have contrasting costumes?

   ....

   ....

Q5 All of the action in the play takes place in the space of one evening.
What are the effects of this? Tick any relevant statements from the list below.

   The action feels more realistic because the audience is watching it in real time. ☐

   It increases tension because the play is always focused on the crisis unfolding in the house. ☐

   The audience must rely on other characters for information about Eva/Daisy's past. ☐

   Small changes in mood are felt more easily. ☐

This is all good to consider — just don't lose the plot...

Using your answer to Q1, create a different setting for *An Inspector Calls*. You can be as creative as
you like — as long as you keep the same atmosphere. Write a paragraph explaining your choice.

Dramatic Techniques

Q1   What makes the end of Act One a cliffhanger?

....

....

Q2   How does Priestley structure Gerald's confession to the Inspector in Act Two
in order to keep the audience in suspense about his affair with Eva/Daisy?

....

....

Q3   The audience is never shown the photograph of Eva/Daisy
used by the Inspector. What effect does this have?

....

....

Q4   The Inspector conducts his investigation "**one line of inquiry at a time.**"
Explain how this helps to build tension in the play.

....

....

....

Q5   Priestley uses the entrances and exits of characters to create certain effects. Explain the effect of:

a) Sheila running offstage when the Inspector shows her the photograph (Act One).

....

....

b) Eric's reappearance at the end of Act Two.

....

....

Q6 Read the paragraph below and fill in the gaps using words from the box.

In the play, noises are used to increase tension. The offstage sounds of the

.... slamming and the doorbell ringing make the

.... wonder who is entering and exiting the house.

This creates suspense. As the plot unfolds, the .... of the

characters' .... changes. It becomes sharper and the

characters begin to shout. This helps to build ....

| slang |
| audience |
| tone |
| dialogue |
| tension |
| gate |
| plot |
| door |
| actions |
| Inspector |

Q7 How does the Inspector control the pace of the play? Give two examples.

© Francis Loney/ArenaPAL

1) ....
....

2) ....
....

Q8 Priestley creates different moods in the play.
Find an example of an event in the play where the mood is:

celebratory: ....

sad: ....

threatening: ....

Q9 Explain how *An Inspector Calls* can be seen as:

a) a murder mystery.

....

b) a moral tale.

....

Priestley's dramatic techniques made quite a scene

EXAM PRACTICE

Explain how Priestley builds excitement in the plot of *An Inspector Calls*. Write about
techniques he uses to make it exciting and how they allow him to explore important id

Priestley's Use of Language

Q1 The Birlings use words which show that they are middle class.
Find two examples of middle-class language they use in the play.

1) .... 2) ....

Q2 Priestley often makes the characters interrupt each other and gives them short sentences
to make the dialogue in the play sound like natural speech. What effect does this have?

....

....

Q3 Priestley describes Arthur Birling as being *"rather provincial in his speech"*,
even though he is a wealthy man. What does this suggest about his background?

....

....

Q4 Mrs Birling says that the way the Inspector spoke to them was unlike *"a real police inspector"*.
Explain how the way the Inspector addresses them goes against her expectations.

a) Expectations:

....

b) Reality:

....

....

Q5 How does Sheila's language change over the
course of the play to reflect her changing attitude?

....

....

....

....

© Simon Gough Photography

...restimate language — *it's pretty remarkable...*

...audience a lot about the characters in the play. It also helps link the characters to
... — it can tell you about a character's social class or how much they've learned.

...riter's Techniques

:(☐ :) ☐ ;) ☐

Language Techniques

Q1 Give an example of dramatic irony from one of Arthur's speeches in Act One. Explain how Priestley's use of dramatic irony undermines Arthur's character.

> Dramatic irony is when the audience knows more than the characters.

Quote: ....

Explanation: ....

....

Q2 Gerald and the Birlings use euphemisms in their dialogue. What does this suggest about their attitudes towards unpleasant aspects of real life?

> A euphemism is a way of avoiding saying something unpleasant by using other, often more vague, words.

....

....

Q3 Read the Inspector's final speech in Act Three (**"But just remember this... Good night."**). Find examples of the language techniques below, then give the effect that each one has.

Technique	Example	Effect
Imagery	"they will be taught it in fire and blood and anguish"	
Use of the first-person plural ('we')		
Repetition		

Q4 Why do you think the Inspector describes Eva/Daisy's suicide using graphic imagery?

....

....

....

 EXAM TIP

I'm pretty glad the Inspector's not my teacher...

In the exam, once you've identified a language technique you'll need to give an example identify the effect it has. You'll also have to explain how the language technique creat

Staging and Dramatic Techniques

An Inspector Calls was written to be performed, so it's important to be familiar with the staging and dramatic techniques Priestley uses. On this page you'll practise writing about these aspects of the play. You can quote stage directions in the same way as dialogue to give evidence for your points.

Don't forget to think about the P.E.E.D. structure (see pages 13 and 45 for more on this) — it'll help you to remember to give examples and think about the effects Priestley creates in the play.

Q1 Read Act One of *An Inspector Calls* from where Mrs Birling, Sheila and Eric leave the dining room to where the doorbell rings. Find stage directions which demonstrate the following points and briefly explain them. Use the example below to help you.

Mr Birling wants to impress Gerald

Mr Birling *"lights his cigar"* and offers Gerald the *"decanter"* — cigars and port are signs of wealth.

a) Eric is left out of a joke

....

....

b) Eric is hiding something

....

....

Q2 Mrs Birling speaks *"**haughtily**"* and is *"**annoyed**"* when she is questioned by the Inspector. How do these stage directions add to Priestley's presentation of Mrs Birling?

....

....

....

Q3 Find three stage directions which show how the actor playing the Inspector should deliver his lines. What do they tell you about the Inspector as a character?

.......ons: ....

....

....

riter's Techni

riter's Techniques

Practice Questions

After all that drama, it's time for a change of scene with some classic practice exam questions. Include points about the different techniques Priestley uses in the play to see how well this section has sunk in. Remember to scribble a quick plan for each question before you start, just like you would in the exam.

Q1 Write about the significance of the setting of *An Inspector Calls*.

You should write about:
- the nature of the set and its effects
- how Priestley uses the setting to convey important ideas.

Q2 **"Why — you fool — *he knows*. Of course he knows. And I hate to think how much he knows that we don't know yet."** (Sheila, Act One)

Explore how Priestley creates tension in *An Inspector Calls*.

Q3 Write about Priestley's use of atmosphere in *An Inspector Calls*.

You should write about:
- how Priestley creates atmosphere in the play
- how Priestley uses atmosphere to present ideas about characters and their attitudes.

Q4 Explain how Priestley presents conflict between different characters in the play.

Q5 How does Priestley use the audience's emotions to help him convey important ideas in *An Inspector Calls*?

You should write about:
- how Priestley influences the audience's thoughts and feelings during the play
- how this helps him to convey important ideas.

Section Five — Exam Buster

Understanding the Question

Underline key words in the question

Q1 Underline the most important words in the following questions.
The first one has been done for you.

a) <u>Explain</u> <u>how</u> Priestley <u>presents</u> the theme of <u>judgement</u> in the play.

b) What is the significance of Mr Birling in *An Inspector Calls*?

c) Explain how the theme of family life is explored in *An Inspector Calls*.

d) How is staging used to create suspense in *An Inspector Calls*?

e) Explain how the importance of gender roles is explored in the play.

f) How is the character of Mrs Birling presented in *An Inspector Calls*?

g) Explain why Eric changes in the play.

Make sure you understand exam language

Q2 Match each exam question to the correct explanation of what you would need to do to answer it. You'll only need to use each white box once.

a) Explain how Priestley presents the theme of judgement in the play.	**1)** Analyse how a character contributes to the action and overall message of the play.
b) What is the significance of Mr Birling in *An Inspector Calls*?	**2)** Analyse how Priestley writes about a character.
c) Explain how the importance of gender roles is explored in the play.	**3)** Analyse the reasons for a development or event in the text.
d) How is the character of Mrs Birling presented in *An Inspector Calls*?	**4)** Analyse how a theme contributes to the action and overall message of the play.
e) Explain why Eric changes in the play.	**5)** Analyse how Priestley writes about a theme in the play.

Exam language — mainly just sighs of despair...

No matter how keen you might be to start your essay, make sure you read the question several times and think about exactly what you're being asked to do. You don't want to end up writing about the wrong thing...

Making a Rough Plan

Jot down your main ideas

Q1 Look at the exam question below, then complete the spider diagram with at least three more main points for answering it.

Don't forget to underline the key words in the question before you start.

Eva/Daisy is presented as a victim of the class system.

Write about how Priestley explores the theme of social class in *An Inspector Calls*.

Put your best points and examples in a logical order

Q2 Choose your three best points from Q1 and fill in the plan below, adding evidence (a quote or an example from the play) for each point.

(Introduction)

Point One: ....

Evidence: ....

Point Two: ....

Evidence: ....

Point Three: ....

Evidence: ....

(Conclusion)

Don't jump to conclusions — plan your essay carefully...

A plan is your friend. It'll help you stay focused under pressure, stop you going off track and reass͟͟͟͟
start to panic. And it only takes five minutes of your time — I'm sure you can spare that for such

Making Links

Make links with other parts of the text

Q1 Look at the exam question and the table below. Complete the table with other relevant parts of the text which could be used to back up each point.

> Write about how Priestley explores the idea of a conflict between the generations in the play.

Point	Example 1	Example 2
Arthur and Sybil have traditional views.	Arthur wants to protect Sheila from unpleasant topics.	
Sheila challenges her parents' authority.	She tells her father not to interfere.	
Gerald is young but shares the views of the older generation.	He agrees with Mr Birling's sacking of Eva/Daisy.	

Extend your essay with other examples

You won't have time to do really detailed planning in the exam so you should get into the habit of quickly thinking of links when you're doing practice questions.

Q2 Look back at the points you included in your plan in Q2 on p.43. For each point, write down another example from a different part of the text that you could include in your essay.

Example for Point One: ....

....

Example for Point Two: ....

....

....l.. for Point Three: ....

....

...ure you if you a good friend...

...e — Exam Bus

age, you may also like page 22...

...nt parts of the text will make your answer more convincing and show that you have ...play. It's a lot easier to do this if you're really familiar with the text, so get reading...

Buster

Structuring Your Answer

P.E.E.D. stands for Point, Example, Explain, Develop

Q1   Read the following extract from an exam answer. Label each aspect of P.E.E.D.

> Gerald shares many of Arthur Birling's views, particularly about business. For example, his statement that Arthur "couldn't have done anything else" with regards to sacking Eva Smith shows that, like Arthur, he also lacks social responsibility and thinks that it's acceptable to prioritise profit over his employees' well-being. The similarity between Gerald and Mr Birling is also shown at the end of the play, when they are both happy to believe that it was all a hoax.

Embedding quotes is a great way to give evidence

Q2   Rewrite the following sentences so that a short part of the quote is embedded in each one.

a)   Eric doesn't like what his parents have done. — "I'm ashamed of you"

....

b)   Mr Birling is worried. — "There'll be a public scandal."

....

Structure your answer using the P.E.E.D. method

Q3   Use the P.E.E.D. method to structure a paragraph on your first point from Q2 on page 43.

Point: ....

....

Example: ....

....

Explain: ....

....

Develop: ....

....

Surely you didn't think I'd stoop that low...

This is a serious and important topic in a serious and important publication — it's no place for toil(Tee hee.) Using the P.E.E.D. method will make sure your paragraphs are beautifully clear and s

Introductions and Conclusions

Give a clear answer to the question in your introduction

Q1 Read the question and the introduction extracts below. Decide which is better and explain why.

> How is the character of Arthur Birling used to present ideas about social responsibility in the play?

a)

Social responsibility is a really important theme in *An Inspector Calls*. The theme is presented by lots of different characters and events, and Arthur Birling is in the middle of this. He has no social responsibility and is an unpleasant character. Also, he doesn't get on with his son Eric and tries to impress Gerald, who belongs to a higher social class.

b)

Arthur Birling is central to Priestley's presentation of ideas about social responsibility. He represents what Priestley saw as the middle class's disregard for the working class. Arthur is a hard-headed businessman who is more interested in profit than in his employees' welfare. The devastating consequences of this attitude are shown by the death of Eva/Daisy.

Better intro: .... Reason: ....

....

....

....

Don't write any new points in your conclusion

Q2 Read the conclusion to the exam question in Q1, then say how it could be improved.

> In conclusion, Arthur Birling isn't a likeable character. He doesn't care about how his actions affect others, so he has no social responsibility. Another important point is that his business views are the opposite of Priestley's socialist beliefs — he wants to work with Gerald's father to achieve "lower costs".

....

....

....

....

....

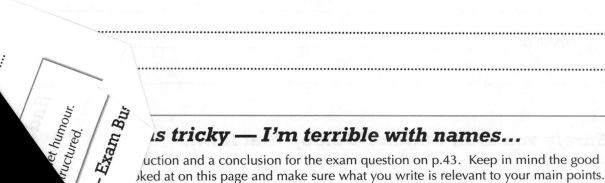

...s tricky — I'm terrible with names...

...uction and a conclusion for the exam question on p.43. Keep in mind the good ...ked at on this page and make sure what you write is relevant to your main points.

...uster

Writing about Context

Make sure you can link the play to its context

Q1 Match each event with the relevant contextual information.

> **a)** As a wealthy business owner, Arthur is able to sack workers for speaking out and asking for higher wages.

> **b)** In an attempt to win over Gerald and his family, Arthur says that he may receive a knighthood.

> **c)** Mrs Birling explains to Sheila that Gerald will sometimes be busy with work, and she must get used to it.

> **1)** Social position was considered to be very important at the time when *An Inspector Calls* is set.

> **2)** Priestley believed that power and wealth were shared out unequally in society.

> **3)** At the start of the 20th century, most middle- and upper-class men were expected to provide for their families.

Include context in your answer

Q2 Read the sample answer below and underline the contextual information.
Then write a paragraph using your second point from page 43 and
include contextual information of your own. Use the P.E.E.D. method.

> As a wealthy business owner, Arthur Birling has considerable power and influence over the lives of other people. For example, he was able to sack Eva Smith for her role in the strike. Eva lost her job for speaking out and asking for higher wages, which sparked an unfortunate chain of events in which her existence became increasingly precarious. This reflects Priestley's belief that power and wealth were shared out unequally in society in the early 20th century. Through Eva/Daisy's death, he shows the disastrous consequences that a power imbalance can have.

....

....

....

....

....

....

In 1912, no one had to sit GCSE English Literature exams...

You'll impress the examiner if you can make links between events in the play and its context. For example, one way to do this is by writing about how the social expectations of the time influence the characters' behaviour.

Linking Ideas and Paragraphs

Link your ideas so your argument is easy to follow

Q1   Rewrite the sample answer below, adding words and/or phrases so the ideas are clearly linked.

> Sheila challenges her parents' views. Mr and Mrs Birling are relieved that there is no Inspector Goole on the police force. Sheila says sarcastically that they are "all nice people" again. She knows that they have still made terrible mistakes. She wants her parents to realise this.

....

....

....

....

....

Q2   Write a paragraph using your third point from p.43. Make sure your ideas are properly connected.

....

....

....

....

....

Show how your paragraphs follow on from each other

Q3   Look at the three paragraphs you have written on pages 45, 47 and in Q2 on this page.
Write down linking words or phrases you could use to link them together in your answer.

Paragraphs to link	Linking word or phrase
p.45 and p.47	
p.47 and p.48	

Click on this <u>link</u> for guaranteed exam success...*

No one is trying to catch you out in the exam, so don't panic. Make sure you read the question carefully and please, *please* spend five minutes planning — it'll help you no end.

*Easy way out currently unavailable due to technical problems

Marking Answer Extracts

Get familiar with the mark scheme

Grade band	An answer at this level...
8-9	• shows an insightful and critical personal response to the text • closely and perceptively analyses how the writer uses language, form and structure to create meaning and affect the reader, making use of highly relevant subject terminology • supports arguments with well-integrated, highly relevant and precise examples from the text • gives a detailed exploration of the relationship between the text and its context • uses highly varied vocabulary and sentence types, with mostly accurate spelling and punctuation
6-7	• shows a critical and observant personal response to the text • includes a thorough exploration of how the writer uses language, form and structure to create meaning and affect the reader, making use of appropriate subject terminology • supports arguments with integrated, well-chosen examples from the text • explores the relationship between the text and its context • uses a substantial range of vocabulary and sentence types, with generally accurate spelling and punctuation
4-5	• shows a thoughtful and clear personal response to the text • examines how the writer uses language, form and structure to create meaning and affect the reader, making some use of relevant subject terminology • integrates appropriate examples from the text • shows an understanding of contextual factors • uses a moderate range of vocabulary and sentence types, without spelling and punctuation errors which make the meaning unclear

Have a go at marking an answer extract

Q1 Using the mark scheme, put the sample answer extract below in a grade band and explain why.

> Explain how Priestley presents the character of Eric in *An Inspector Calls*.

> Eric is presented as an outsider in Birling family life. At the begining of the play, he is described as *"not quite at ease"*, and he laughs for no reason. Priestly uses him to show that the Birlings are not a really happy family. Also his langage when he talks about Eva/Daisy shows that he is insensitive — he describes her as "a good sport". Priestly uses Eric to show that the class system was unfair because the higher classes weren't as moral as people thought.

Grade band: .... Reason: ....

....

....

....

Marking Answer Extracts

Have a look at these extracts from answers to the question on page 49

Q1 For each extract, say what grade band you think it is in, then underline an example of where it meets each of the mark scheme criteria. Label each underlined point to show what it achieves.

---

a) Priestley uses stage directions to present Eric as a challenge to the illusion of respectable middle-class family life. Eric disrupts the polite conversation when he "*suddenly guffaws*" and talks "*rather noisily*". Eric's inappropriate laughter and loud speech imply that he is uncomfortable in the situation, which suggests that problems lurk beneath the decorous surface of Birling family life.

The way Eric's language changes depending on his audience suggests that his polite middle-class behaviour is only superficial. When discussing his involvement with Eva/Daisy in front of his mother and sister, he says he was "in that state when a chap easily turns nasty", meaning that he was drunk and aggressive. He uses euphemism to avoid the horror of what he has done, which suggests a lack of honesty in middle-class family life. In contrast, when the women have left, he uses more direct, vulgar language, scorning the "fat old tarts" in the town. The speed of this change shows how quickly the impression of respectability crumbles. Priestley's presentation of Eric also demonstrates that people of a higher class did not automatically have higher morals, which in turn highlights the injustice of the rigid class system of the time which benefited those at the top.

Grade band: ....

---

b) One of the main purposes of the character of Eric is to show the immoral side of the middle class. Priestley achieves this by revealing that Eric drunkenly forced himself on Eva/Daisy. Eric's appalling treatment of Eva/Daisy sharply contrasts with the image of the perfect family that Arthur Birling wants to create, suggesting that the idea of middle-class respectability is false. Priestley's negative portrayal of Eric demonstrates that there is no connection between social status and morality, which goes against accepted beliefs in the early 20th century.

However, Priestley also presents Eric as troubled and sensitive. This idea is developed through his difficult relationship with his mother, who Eric sees as responsible for the death of his child. The strength of Eric's feelings of resentment and frustration is shown through his disrupted, repetitive speech, for example when he tells her "you killed her — and the child she'd have had too — my child". His youthful anger makes him seem vulnerable. Eric feels misunderstood by his family, believing that Mrs Birling "never even tried" to understand. This makes the audience feel sympathy for Eric, despite his unprincipled actions.

Grade band: ....

Marking a Whole Answer

Now try marking this whole answer

Q1 Read the sample answer below. On page 52, put it in a grade band and explain your decision.

> How is the theme of men and women explored in *An Inspector Calls*?

If it helps you, label examples of where the answer meets the mark scheme criteria.

In *An Inspector Calls*, Priestley explores the differing treatment people often receive based on their gender, and how this makes life particularly difficult for working-class women. The play also explores how men and women act towards each other and shows that the men's actions are often contradictory. For example, Gerald believes men should protect women, but he exploits Eva/Daisy. In addition, Priestley explores the gender roles which existed at the start of the 20th century and shows them to be unfair. Sheila and Eva/Daisy both try to break away from the rules dictated to them by society, but this has disastrous consequences for Eva/Daisy. This suggests that gender roles are both deeply ingrained in society and can be highly damaging.

Through his portrayal of Eva/Daisy, Priestley shows that young, working-class women are disadvantaged. Eva Smith's name implies that she represents all working-class women. "Eva" is similar to Eve, the first woman according to many religious traditions, and "Smith" is a common surname and is also a kind of tradesman, so she represents the working class. The difficulties experienced by working-class women are emphasised by Sheila's accusation that Arthur sees these girls as "cheap labour". This expression dehumanises the people who make up the working class and creates the impression that their individual concerns don't matter. The Inspector makes Eva/Daisy's problems very real for the Birlings and Gerald, and this is why Sheila starts to see the working class as individuals. Telling the story in the form of a play allows Priestley to prevent Eva/Daisy appearing on stage, so the audience only finds out about her through other characters. This lack of a voice could represent her powerlessness and may emphasise how difficult it was for working-class women to establish themselves in a male-dominated, class-ridden society.

The idea of working-class women struggling in life is developed through the Inspector's use of imagery, for example when he suggests that more privileged people ought to put themselves in the place of "young women counting their pennies in their dingy little back bedrooms." The word "pennies" shows their poverty, as pennies were amongst the least valuable coins, and the fact that the women have to count them shows how difficult it is for them to survive. The adjective "dingy" evokes a dirty, dark and unpleasant environment, which adds to the impression of hardship. This powerful image gives a clear sense of how difficult it was for working-class women to survive, and how bleak their existence could be.

Priestley's presentation of the theme of men and women also highlights a contradiction in the way some men behaved towards women in society. The social expectation in the early 20th century, when *An Inspector Calls* is set, was that men ought to protect women, and this is illustrated when Gerald encourages Sheila to leave the room so she won't have to hear about his affair. However, the Inspector reveals the hypocrisy of Gerald's attempt to protect Sheila from an "unpleasant and disturbing" experience by repeating his phrase back to him and then applying it to Eva/Daisy, who wasn't protected from harm. The repetition highlights the inconsistency of Gerald's approach. He has one rule for women of a similar class to him, and another for lower-class women.

This answer continues on p.52. ⟶

Marking a Whole Answer

As well as highlighting the plight of working-class women, Priestley explores the gender roles which existed in middle-class family life in the early 20th century. Mrs Birling tries to impart traditional values on Sheila, telling her that she will have to "get used to" the fact that her husband will often prioritise business over family life. This illustrates the expectation in the 1910s that a middle-class woman would stay at home and look after the family, while a man's main concern should be providing for the family by working. Furthermore, in telling Sheila not to "tease" Gerald, Mrs Birling implies that men know best, and that women should adopt a more submissive role in their relationships.

The play's structure is used to depict the breakdown of these roles. Sheila is only the second member of the family to be questioned by the Inspector — she learns her lesson in Act One. This then allows her to question the actions of her parents later in the play. For example, she criticises Mr Birling's refusal to take responsibility for his actions in Act Three, telling him: "you don't seem to have learnt anything." This contrasts with her submissive attitude towards him at the start of the play. She also shows increasing maturity and is able to learn from the Inspector about the difficulties faced by the working class. The audience realises that she is an intelligent young woman capable of thinking for herself, which challenges the gender roles that existed at the time.

However, it is arguably not clear how much difference this breakdown of gender roles will make to the characters in the long term. The strength of social expectations about men and women is demonstrated when Gerald asks Sheila, "What about this ring?" Although Sheila has clearly changed her attitude and become more mature and independent, it is still expected that she will get married and rely on her husband. Eva/Daisy's fate suggests that it could even be dangerous for women to be too independent: she tried to make her own way in life and ended up dying a painful, tragic death.

Priestley's exploration of the theme of men and women is complex. Gender roles influence how the characters behave towards one another and the sense of Eva/Daisy's exploitation by men runs throughout the play. Priestley depicts behaviour which conforms to social expectations, such as Mrs Birling's, and behaviour which challenges expectations, such as Sheila's. However, Priestley ultimately shows how deeply ingrained gender roles are. The characters' revelations suggest to the audience that Eva/Daisy was an independent-minded, strong-willed person, yet she meets a tragic end. Therefore, any audience viewing *An Inspector Calls* will be left with a strong sense of the injustice of gender inequality.

Grade band: .... Reasons: ....

....

....

....

....

Mark schemes — he's always got a cunning plan...

If you're really familiar with the mark scheme for your exam board, you'll know exactly what the examiner is looking for. You're being tested on several skills, so you'll need to demonstrate all of them to get top marks.

Writing Well

Spelling, punctuation and grammar (SPaG for short) might not be the most exciting things in the world, but in the exam marks will be awarded for good English, so you don't want to miss out. Using a variety of sentence structures and vocabulary will also make your answer more impressive. It's a good idea to leave a few minutes at the end of the exam to check through your work for silly mistakes, like misspelt names. On this page you'll have chance to hone your skills.

Q1 Read the sample answer below. Underline the SPaG mistakes, then correct them. One has already been done for you.

> The audience witnesses the gradual breakdown of the <u>Briling</u>^(Birling) family structure. After
>
> the Inspector leaves in Act Three, Shiela and Eric challenge there parents. Mrs Birling
>
> trys to show that she is in charge, telling sheila not to be "childish", but Sheila replies,
>
> "it's you to who are being childish. Sheila disagrees with how her parent's are behaving.

Q2 Rewrite the following sentences, using appropriate language for the exam.

a) The Inspector seems a bit odd and no one has any idea where he's from.

....

....

b) Mrs Birling is a horrible lady who treats Eva/Daisy like dirt.

....

....

c) The Birlings are always shouting and getting mad at each other.

....

....

d) I reckon that staging is really important for making the play exciting.

....

....

Section Five — Exam Buster

Practice Questions

Now you've polished your essay-writing skills, have a bash at doing these practice questions under exam conditions. Spend five minutes doing a rough plan and about 40 minutes writing your essay. Use the techniques you've learnt in this section and leave a bit of time to check through your answer at the end.

Q1 How does Priestley create a sense of mystery in *An Inspector Calls*?

You should write about:
- how Priestley uses the play's structure to create a sense of mystery
- other aspects of the play which contribute to the sense of mystery.

Q2 How is the character of Eva/Daisy used to explore ideas about prejudice in *An Inspector Calls*?

Q3 How is the character of Arthur Birling used to present ideas about family life in *An Inspector Calls*?

You should write about:
- how Arthur Birling behaves towards his family
- how and why Arthur's position in the family changes throughout the play.

Q4 **"You're just the kind of son-in-law I always wanted."** (Mr Birling, Act One)

Write about how the character of Gerald is used to explore the social context of *An Inspector Calls*.

Q5 What can the audience learn from the Birling family about social responsibility?

Answers

Section One — Analysis of Acts

Page 2: Act One — The Birlings are celebrating

1. a) True: e.g. "the same port your father gets"
   b) True: e.g. "Yes, that's what *you* say."
   c) False: e.g. *"not quite at ease"*
2. a) E.g. "lower costs and higher prices"
   b) E.g. "What an expression, Sheila!"
3. Gerald's mother comes from an old family who own land. She might think Gerald could have done better than Sheila.
4. "a man has to mind his own business and look after himself and his own — and —"
   E.g. It creates the impression that the Inspector has been sent to show Arthur that his uncaring ways are wrong.

Page 3: Act One — The investigation starts

1. The statements should be numbered 2, 6, 3, 1, 4, 5.
2. E.g. He believes that his actions were justified in the interest of business; he claims that he has a "duty to keep labour costs down."
3. E.g. It is troubled. Mr Birling thinks that Eric is spoilt and irresponsible. Eric disagrees with his father's approach to business.
4. a) E.g. He becomes defensive.
      E.g. "there's nothing mysterious — or scandalous — about this business"
   b) He agrees with it.
      E.g. "I know we'd have done the same thing."
   c) She regrets her behaviour.
      E.g. "I'll never, never do it again to anybody."

Page 4: Act One — Gerald becomes involved

1. At first Gerald is confident and he argues with the Inspector. However, when he hears the name 'Daisy Renton', he is shocked and has a drink to calm down.
2. At the beginning of Act One, Sheila talks to Gerald *"gaily, possessively"* and is *"half playful"*, even though she is suspicious about what he was doing the summer before. By the end of the act, she is less playful and more assertive with him: "No, that's no use." She calls Gerald a "fool" and challenges him.
3. a) E.g. "We can't leave it at that."
   b) E.g. "I don't come into this suicide business."
   c) E.g. "Why — you fool — *he knows*."
4. It ends with a question to leave the audience in suspense. The Inspector says, "Well?" which makes the audience wonder if Gerald is involved in Eva/Daisy's death, what he will say and how Sheila will react.

Task: Here are some points that you may have included:
- The start of the play shows the family celebrating a happy event: Sheila and Gerald's engagement. Mr Birling is toasting their health and making a speech about the future while the others listen. As Gerald says, they seem to be a "nice well-behaved family".
- Sheila seems to be an obedient daughter and speaks in quite a childish manner: "I'm sorry, Daddy. Actually I was listening."
- By the end of Act One, family tensions have become more obvious, e.g. Eric and Sheila openly disagree with their father's decision to sack Eva Smith, and Eric criticises Sheila's behaviour.

Page 5: Act Two — Gerald's lies are uncovered

1. Sheila feels responsible for Eva Smith's death once she has told her story. She stays so that she can find out more about how the others were involved and share the responsibility with them.
2. E.g. "No, Mother — please!"
3. The statements should be numbered 4, 1, 3, 6, 5, 2.
4. She thinks that they have changed too much. They would have to start from scratch and get to know each other again.
5. keen, sarcastic, honest, disgusting, common
   (Other answers are also possible.)

Page 6: Act Two — Sybil won't accept responsibility

1. The statements should be numbered 2, 4, 3, 5, 6, 1.
2. E.g. Eva/Daisy called herself "Mrs Birling" when she went to ask for help, which Sybil considered a "gross impertinence". Sybil also found out that Eva/Daisy's story about having a husband was "quite false".
3. Sybil is unkind and unsympathetic because she wouldn't help someone in need. She is arrogant because she thinks that her opinion is the only one that matters.
4. a) E.g. "I've done nothing wrong"
   b) E.g. "I think you did something terribly wrong"

Page 7: Act Two — The Inspector catches Sybil out

1. a) True: "alone, friendless, almost penniless, desperate."
   b) False: "Mother, I think it was cruel and vile."
   c) True: e.g. "The Press might easily take it up"
2. The Inspector knows Eric is the father of Eva/Daisy's child. Once Sybil has blamed the father, the Inspector asks her what should be done with him, knowing that she will condemn her own son.
3. Eva/Daisy suspected that the money was stolen.
4. a) He should take responsibility for his actions in public.
      E.g. "He should be made an example of"
   b) She starts to panic.
      E.g. "Mother — stop — stop!"

Task: Here are some points you may have included:
- Act One: the speech Arthur makes just before the Inspector arrives. He says "a man has to mind his own business and look after himself". This is significant because it shows that he has an uncaring attitude towards others. Also, the Inspector arrives immediately afterwards so it seems as though Arthur has summoned him with his words. This suggests that the Inspector will try to challenge his views.
- Act Two: when Sheila stands up to Gerald and insists on staying to hear the rest of the investigation. This is an important event because it shows that Sheila is becoming more independent. We also see further cracks in their relationship when Gerald says, "So that's what you think I'm really like."

Page 8: Act Three — It's Eric's turn to be questioned

1. Eric enters at the end of Act Two, looking *"distressed"*, but then the curtain falls, so everyone is left in suspense. At the start of Act Three everyone is still *"staring"* at him, which adds tension — the characters and audience are all waiting for a revelation.
2. a) Mrs Birling — She's shocked that Eric is the father.
   b) The Inspector — He's impatient with Mr Birling.
3. Eric was very worried. He says that he was "in a hell of a state about it". He and Daisy discussed marriage, but she didn't want to marry him.
4. a) "you're not the kind of father a chap could go to when he's in trouble"
   b) E.g. "you killed her — and the child she'd have had too"
   c) "You don't understand anything. You never did. You never even tried"

Page 9: Act Three — The Inspector gives his verdict

1. a) Mrs Birling   b) Eric   c) Mr Birling
2. All of humanity is connected, so our actions have an impact on other people's lives. There are lots of people who need help and it is our responsibility to look after them.
3. a) "There'll be a public scandal."
   b) "I behaved badly too. I know I did. I'm ashamed of it."
   c) "What does it matter now whether they give you a knighthood or not?"
4. You should say who you agree with, how they react, and why you think they are right to behave like this.
   E.g. I agree with Sheila's reaction the most. She accepts responsibility for her part in Eva/Daisy's death, saying that she

is "ashamed", and she wants her parents to learn from their mistakes too.

Page 10: Act Three — The Birlings can't agree

1. Sheila, the Inspector, Mr Birling, Sheila and Eric (either way around), Mr Birling, Sheila and Eric (either way around), the Inspector
2. Whether there really was a suicide that day; If the Inspector was a real police inspector; How much the Inspector knew in advance
3. There is no police officer called Goole on the force.
4. Mr Birling quickly accepts the idea, speaking *"eagerly"* and agreeing that there "wasn't the slightest proof" that she was just one girl. Eric thinks that it doesn't make a difference because the girl he knew "is dead".
5. Mr Birling — He is relieved.
   Sheila — She is still upset about the family's behaviour.

Page 11: Act Three — The play ends with a twist

1. a) True: e.g. "It frightens me the way you talk."
   b) True: e.g. "Everything's all right now, Sheila."
   c) True: e.g. "In the morning they'll be as amused as we are."
2. The police phone the Birlings to say that an inspector is on his way. This reminds the audience of when Edna announced "an inspector's called".
3. E.g. Gerald, Mr Birling and Mrs Birling will be defensive as they don't think they are responsible. Mrs Birling might ask him "a few questions" to see if he's a real police officer. Sheila and Eric may confess more quickly than the first time.
4. E.g. Yes, because even if the Birlings are not punished by law, they will be punished by a public scandal if the truth is revealed. Also, they will be punished by the negative impact the events have had on their family relationships.
Task: You may have included the following points:
   - Arthur started off the process by sacking her from her job at his factory. This left her unemployed for a while, but she was able to find work in a clothes shop — Milwards.
   - Eva/Daisy lost her job because Sheila complained about her — Sheila abused her position of power as a rich customer. After this, Eva was unable to find employment and became a prostitute.
   - Gerald met Eva/Daisy when she was a prostitute. She became his mistress and was happy for a while. Gerald gave her money to support herself, but ultimately he ended the affair.
   - Eric made things much worse for Eva/Daisy. He forced her to have sex with him and got her pregnant. He offered her help she couldn't accept (stolen money) and she ended up in a desperate situation.
   - Mrs Birling was the last of the family to see Eva/Daisy, and she refused to help her, even though Eva/Daisy was desperate. Eva/Daisy had nowhere left to turn, so she killed herself.
   You should have included a conclusion saying who played the biggest role in Eva/Daisy's death and why. However, you may have argued that no one person can be held responsible because all their actions were linked.

Page 12: Skills Focus — Using Quotes

1. accurate, relevant, irrelevant, embedded, important, repeat
   (Other answers are also possible.)
2. Good quote usage: b) and c) *[relevant and well embedded]*
   Bad quote usage: a) *[irrelevant]*, d) *[repeats point above too closely]* and e) *[too long, not embedded]*
3. You could have rewritten the examples as follows:
   a) The Inspector displays sympathy for Eva/Daisy. He tells the Birlings that someone had made a "nasty mess" of her life and asks them to put themselves in her position.
   d) Mrs Birling believes that the father is "entirely responsible".
   e) In Act Three, Sheila tells her parents that she doesn't want "a nice cosy talk" because she can't just move on like them — she still feels "the same" about what happened.

Page 13: Skills Focus — P.E.E.D.

1. a) The Explain stage is missing. A sentence should be added to explain the quote, for example:
      Here, his language is harsh and graphic, emphasising the suffering Eva/Daisy must have endured. This challenges the Birlings' disregard for the welfare of the working class.
   b) The Example stage is missing. A specific example or a quote should be added to back up the initial statement, for example:
      At the beginning of Act Two, she insists on staying to listen because she wants to learn the truth, even though Gerald thinks it will be "unpleasant and disturbing" for her.
   c) The Develop stage is missing. The answer should be extended by explaining the effect on the audience or linking the example to another aspect of the play, for example:
      To the audience, she appears cruel, small-minded and unaware: she is the one who lacks morality, not Eva/Daisy.

Section Two — Characters

Pages 14-15: The Inspector

1. The Inspector has a powerful presence on stage. He has an air of authority which makes him seem physically bigger than he really is.
2. a) E.g. "I remember... what he made me feel."
   b) E.g. "there was something curious about him"
   c) E.g. "so rude — and assertive"
3. He believes that everybody's lives are intertwined and that all members of society should be responsible for one another. He thinks that being socially responsible, e.g. treating others fairly, can make a real difference to society.
4. true, false, false, true, true
5. The audience thinks that the Inspector is in control. His confidence and authority over the other characters makes him seem powerful and trustworthy.
6. His tactic of questioning them one by one singles out each character, making them more vulnerable. He is also persistent and only moves on to a new question when he's satisfied with the response he's had.
7. E.g. He doesn't let Mr Birling's social connections influence his investigation. / He accuses Mrs Birling of lying.
8. 'Goole' sounds like 'ghoul'. This hints that the Inspector could be supernatural.
9. E.g. No, because Gerald and the Birlings all did something wrong. Even if they aren't being accused of crimes, they should still take responsibility for using their power and social status to mistreat another person. **Or** e.g. Yes, because unless Gerald and the Birlings are made to accept responsibility in public for their actions, it's unlikely that they'll change the way they treat other people.

Page 16: Arthur Birling

1. E.g. selfish, arrogant, anxious
   Any relevant quotes, e.g. "a man has to mind his own business" (selfish) / "it has nothing whatever to do with the wretched girl's suicide" (arrogant) / "Most of this is bound to come out." (anxious)
2. b) He likes to tell other people what he thinks.
   c) He is used to manipulating other people.
   d) He doesn't know as much as he thinks he does.
3. E.g. I think Mr Birling is partly responsible. Sacking her put her in a precarious position, but she did find another job.
4. He is triumphant and relieved, and he sees the Inspector's visit as a joke. This shows that his views haven't changed because he still doesn't think he's done anything wrong.
Task: You should have created a job advertisement based on information given or suggested about Birling and Company in the play. Desirable qualities might include: hard-working, efficient, obedient and skilled. Unsuitable qualities might include: strong-willed, outspoken, independent and assertive.

Answers

Page 17: Sybil Birling

1. Mrs Birling helps to run a women's charity. When Eva/Daisy went to the charity for help, Mrs Birling used her influence to convince the other board members to turn her away.
2. E.g. Because she belongs to the higher classes. Respect and traditional values are an important part of her social identity.
3. E.g. She dislikes Eva/Daisy's "manner" and lets this affect her judgement.
4. She is rude to the Inspector and argues with him. She also tries to assert her power and authority over him.
   Any relevant quote, e.g. "what business is it of yours?"
5. E.g. No, because she clearly cares about her family. She's happy for Sheila at the start of the play and is upset when Eric accuses her of killing his child. **Or** e.g. Yes, because she isn't affectionate towards her children and doesn't feel sorry for Eva/Daisy, even when she learns that she was telling the truth.

Page 18: Sheila Birling

1. intelligent, secret, affair, the Inspector, Eric
   (Other answers are also possible.)
2. E.g. "Mother, she's just died a horrible death"
   Any valid explanation, e.g. It shows she's distressed by Eva/Daisy's death and suggests that she feels sorry for Eva/Daisy.
3. Before he arrives, she's immature and shallow. She uses childish language and is distracted by her engagement ring. After he leaves, she's more mature, having realised the effect that her actions can have on other people.
4. E.g. No, because Gerald has betrayed her. After Gerald admits his affair, Sheila realises "You and I aren't the same people who sat down to dinner". **Or** e.g. Yes, because young women were expected to marry. Sheila was also very excited about her engagement at the start of the play.
Task: You should have written your letter from Sheila's point of view. Here are some points you may have included:
   - The Inspector showed that the Birlings' decision to judge Eva/Daisy based on her class was misguided. The Birlings' actions towards Eva/Daisy were motivated by prejudice and ignorance. Eva/Daisy proved those prejudices wrong — she worked hard and was moral.
   - The Inspector taught the Birlings that they have a duty to look after others in society by showing them how their actions impact other people. Eva/Daisy's death showed the Birlings that their position as a middle-class family gives them power over the lives of the lower class and that they shouldn't abuse that power.
   - Eva/Daisy's death wasn't just an unfortunate coincidence. The Inspector said there are "millions of Eva Smiths and John Smiths still left with us". Unless Mr and Mrs Birling's attitudes change, they'll continue to damage the lives of others.

Page 19: Eric Birling

1. To suggest that he doesn't quite fit in with the rest of the family. This makes the audience suspicious.
2. a) E.g. "You don't understand anything."
   b) E.g. "she was... a good sport"
3. Eric continues to feel guilty and ashamed while Mr and Mrs Birling are relieved and begin to see the evening's events as a joke.
4. E.g. Eric, because he forces Eva/Daisy to have sex, but is unable to support her when she falls pregnant. Unlike Gerald, he doesn't ever care much about her. **Or** e.g. Gerald, because he isn't as naive as Eric. He's aware of how ending the affair might affect Eva/Daisy, but this doesn't change how he treats her.
5. E.g. I disagree. The play suggests that what Eric did wasn't unusual. Eric has seen Mr Birling's friends with "tarts", he and Gerald both go to the Palace Bar and Alderman Meggarty is called a known "womanizer". **Or** e.g. I agree. Mrs Birling seems shocked when Eric reveals he forced Eva/Daisy to have sex and Mr Birling is worried that Eric's actions will cause a scandal.

Task: If you argued that Priestley doesn't want the audience to forgive Eric, here are some points you might have included:
   - Priestley presents Eric as a villain in the play. His motives for sleeping with Eva/Daisy are selfish and shallow, and the money he gives to her is stolen. Even though Eric is sorry, the Inspector states "you can't do her any good now", suggesting his regrets are too little, too late.
   - Eric risks severe consequences for his actions. As Mr Birling states, "If anyone's up to the neck in this business, you are". Eric's actions could cause a public scandal and he is guilty of theft. This gives the audience the impression that Eric deserves to be punished rather than forgiven.

Or, if you argued that Priestley does want the audience to forgive Eric, here are some points you might have included:
   - At the end of the play, it's clear that Eric regrets what he has done and feels guilty for his part in Eva/Daisy's death. This helps the audience to forgive him because he seems to have learnt from his mistakes, unlike his parents and Gerald.
   - Priestley presents Eric as a lonely and neglected young man. Eric tells Mr Birling "you're not the kind of father a chap could go to when he's in trouble". This introduces a childish and vulnerable side to Eric's character, which makes his mistakes seem more understandable.

Page 20: Gerald Croft

1. Good: e.g. He takes pity on Eva/Daisy and finds her somewhere to live. "I made her go to Morgan Terrace because I was sorry for her"
   Bad: e.g. He refuses to accept the Inspector's message. "Everything's all right now"
2. Gerald is upper class — if he marries Sheila, the Birlings' social status will improve. The Crofts also own a competing business, so marriage could lead to a business partnership.
3. E.g. "Getting a bit heavy-handed, aren't you, Inspector?"
   Any valid explanation, e.g. Gerald believes that the Inspector is socially inferior to him and wants him to show more respect.
4. Gerald tries to return the situation to how it was at the beginning of the play. He has a drink with Mr Birling and offers Sheila her engagement ring back.

Exam Practice:
Your answer should have an introduction, several paragraphs developing different ideas and a conclusion. You may have included some of the following points:
   - Their relationship reveals Gerald's inability to change. His attempt to reinstate their engagement and his belief that "Everything's all right now" demonstrate his desire to return everything to the way it was before the Inspector arrived. The widening rift between Gerald and Sheila also highlights his association with the members of the older generation, who fail to understand and learn from the Inspector.
   - Priestley uses their relationship to show how Sheila matures over the course of the play. When she receives her engagement ring, she states "Look — Mummy — isn't it a beauty?" Priestley uses hyphens to break up her dialogue into short chunks, giving the impression that she is almost breathless with excitement. Sheila also reverts to calling Mrs Birling "Mummy", which gives her speech a childish tone. This contrasts with the calm and practical tone she adopts when she returns the ring to Gerald: "just in case you forget... I think you'd better take this". This maturity also reveals how she has outgrown the female stereotype of obedience that she embodied at the start of the play.
   - The deterioration of their relationship shows that the Birlings' attempts to ignore unpleasant truths are futile. In Act One, Sheila pushes aside her concerns about Gerald having an affair when she's presented with her ring. However, after Gerald's confession, she admits "I knew anyhow you were lying about those months" — the Inspector has forced her to confront the truth. Her comment to Mr Birling that "Gerald knows what I mean and apparently you don't" reveals the

Answers

growing divide between Sheila and her parents and suggests that the Birlings' pretence of a 'happy family' is no longer sustainable.

Page 21: Eva Smith / Daisy Renton

1. E.g. Mr Birling: "She'd had a lot to say — far too much" / Sheila: "She was a very pretty girl" / Gerald: "she'd been happier than she'd ever been" / Mrs Birling: "She was giving herself ridiculous airs." / Eric: "she wasn't the usual sort."

2. The adjectives should all relate to quotes given in the previous question, e.g. confident, attractive, lonely, different.

3. It makes the audience feel sympathetic towards Eva/Daisy.

4. Priestley doesn't give Eva/Daisy a voice in the play and she never appears on stage. This represents the lack of control she had over her own life as a working-class woman.

5. She is a symbol for all working-class women. This is suggested in her name, which sounds like Eve (the first woman in the Bible) and uses the common surname 'Smith'. Her story could have been pieced together from many different girls and the Inspector claims that "millions of Eva Smiths" are "still left with us".

6. Your timeline should include:
   • August-September 1910 — Eva and her colleagues ask for a pay rise, then go on strike.
   • End of September 1910 — Eva is sacked by Mr Birling.
   • December 1910 — Eva gets a new job at Milwards.
   • End of January 1911 — Eva is sacked from Milwards. She changes her name to Daisy Renton.
   • March 1911 — Daisy meets Gerald at the Palace Bar.
   • September 1911 — Gerald ends the affair with Daisy. Daisy goes away to the seaside for two months.
   • November 1911 — She meets Eric in the Palace Bar.
   • Around the first two months of 1912 — She finds out she is pregnant. She refuses Eric's money and stops seeing him.
   • Around March 1912 — She goes to the charity as "Mrs Birling" for help. Sybil Birling ensures she is turned away.
   • Around March 1912 — She kills herself.

Page 22: Skills Focus — Making Links

1. You could have used the following examples:
   Arthur — He boasts about his connection with influential people such as the Chief Constable. / He worries that Eric's behaviour will cause a scandal.
   Eva/Daisy — She is sacked from the factory for speaking out. / She can't get another job after being forced to leave Milwards.
   Sheila — She knows that Alderman Meggarty is a womanizer. / She realises that Gerald enjoyed Daisy Renton's devotion and dependence.

2. You could have made the following points:
   Sybil — She refuses to change, e.g. When she is being questioned by the Inspector, she avoids taking responsibility and blames the father instead. / She makes light of the events at the end of the play and wants to move on.
   Eric — He ignores middle-class etiquette, e.g. He is drunk at Sheila and Gerald's engagement party. / He shouts at his mother and criticises her for neglecting him.
   The Inspector — He has radical ideas for the time, e.g. He tells the Birlings to put themselves in the place of poor labourers. / He talks about sex and politics when women are present.

Page 23: Practice Questions

Your answers should have an introduction, several paragraphs developing different ideas and a conclusion. You may have included some of the following points:

1. • The Inspector is presented as a figure of moral authority in the play. He judges and scolds Gerald and the Birlings in his final speech, telling them to "remember" his message. His repetition of the first-person plural "we" emphasises that his message is universal, as he is addressing the audience as well as the characters. This makes his speech seem like a sermon, creating an impression of power. It is as though the Inspector

has a god-given authority to decide right from wrong. This encourages the audience to trust the Inspector above the other characters.
   • The language the Inspector uses to address Gerald and the Birlings helps to assert his authority over them. He orders them around, telling them to "be quiet" and to "listen to me." This shows the audience that the Inspector is in control and suggests he doesn't respect the authority granted to Gerald and the Birlings by their social status. Stage directions showing how the actor should speak also show the Inspector's authority — he speaks *massively*, *impressively* and *sternly*.
   • The Inspector's knowledge of events adds to his authority in the play. Gerald and the Birlings are unable to hide the truth from him, and he keeps the audience in suspense by slowly revealing what he and the others know about Eva/Daisy. This presents the Inspector to the audience as a source of authority, as they are dependent on him for information about Eva/Daisy. It also establishes the Inspector's authority over the play as a whole, as the Inspector controls the pace of the action.

2. • Sheila becomes less ignorant over the course of the play. She justifies getting Eva/Daisy dismissed from Milwards because she "looked as if she could take care of herself". This assumption makes Sheila seem naive, as Priestley structures the play so that her confession comes after the audience have heard that Eva/Daisy was sacked from Mr Birling's works and later killed herself. By the end of the play, Priestley shows her to be independent and intelligent. She even recognises the ignorance of others, saying that Mrs Birling hasn't "learnt anything". This helps to highlight the generational divide that Priestley has established.
   • Sheila becomes more assertive throughout the play. At the beginning, she isn't able to argue her own opinions, but as the play progresses, Sheila becomes increasingly confident. She interrupts her mother and father, mocks their views and challenges their authority — "You began to learn something. And now you've stopped." The short sentences make her dialogue concise and direct; this shows the audience she is now confident in opposing her parents' views. Her use of "began" and "stopped" in such close proximity also emphasises how little she thinks her parents have changed. Priestley uses Sheila's disagreement with her parents to give the audience hope that people can change — despite their social class.
   • Sheila also becomes more mature during the play. In Act One, Priestley presents her as childish. She calls her parents "Mummy" and "Daddy", is excitable and sits admiring her engagement ring. As the play progresses, she moves away from being associated with childishness. She refuses to be shielded from "unpleasant and disturbing things" like Gerald's affair, and deals with them in a calm and accepting manner, showing how mature she has become. This attitude creates a contrast with her parents, who stubbornly refuse to face up to the truth.

3. • Mrs Birling's role in Eva/Daisy's death is used by Priestley to reveal class prejudices. Mrs Birling judges whether Eva/Daisy is "deserving" of help using her preconceptions about the working class, saying "As if a girl of that sort would ever refuse money!" By referring to Eva/Daisy euphemistically as "a girl of that sort", Mrs Birling shows that she is unable to put her class prejudices aside and view her as a real person. The exclamatory phrase "As if... !" also stresses to the audience that she is mocking Eva/Daisy, which encourages them to dislike Mrs Birling and the views she represents. As a result, the play dismisses the middle-class view of the time that people in a lower class were morally inferior.
   • Priestley uses Mrs Birling to show how members of the higher classes have mistaken beliefs about the morality of their own class. The play's structure means that Mrs Birling is interviewed before Eric, which allows the Inspector to trick her into condemning her own son. The revelation that her

son is the "drunken young idler" that got Eva/Daisy pregnant highlights the fact that her belief that higher classes have higher morals is wrong. This also encourages the audience to consider their own attitudes towards class, which is one of the main purposes of the play.

- Mrs Birling's character shows that class prejudices hinder change. Her preoccupation with middle-class values means that she can't imagine events from another point of view. She doesn't think "for a moment" that they can understand Eva/Daisy's situation Her inability to empathise means that she can't relate to the Inspector's message and therefore doesn't change at the end of the play. Priestley uses this to show that the class prejudices of the older generation in the play are too ingrained — instead he encourages the audience to put their faith in the younger generation.

4.
- Priestley shows that Eric and Mr Birling can't relate easily to one another, which highlights Mr Birling's lack of empathy. Mr Birling's assertion that "Apparently nothing matters to you" shows that he is unable to accept that Eric has any values, as they don't match his own. This is also reflected in Mr Birling's closer relationship with Gerald, whose like-minded business ideas make him "just the kind of son-in-law" Mr Birling has always wanted.
- At the end of the play, Mr Birling and Eric's relationship is at its worst. Eric tells Mr Birling "I don't give a damn now whether I stay here or not." Priestley uses stage directions to indicate that this should be said "*quietly, bitterly*", which creates a contrast with his preceding dialogue, where he is "*shouting*". The sudden change in volume makes Eric's threat to leave sound sinister and serious. It shows how little Eric relates to his parents and their class attitudes after the Inspector's visit. This forms part of the generational divide at the end of the play, where Sheila and Eric are the only ones shown to have the capacity to change.
- Mr Birling doesn't respect his son's opinions, which highlights his own arrogance. He lectures Eric throughout the play and labels his opinions as "Rubbish!" when they contradict his own beliefs. The word "Rubbish!" is rude and dismissive, suggesting that Mr Birling has an exaggerated sense of self-importance. Priestley presents this attitude as negative by showing that Mr Birling's arrogance prevents him from learning from the Inspector.

5.
- The character of Eva/Daisy is hugely important to Priestley's message in the play. The Inspector uses her as a symbol of all working-class women, telling the Birlings that there are "millions of Eva Smiths" still alive. His statement shows them that they have a responsibility to look after others in society, and that Eva/Daisy could have been only one of many people they have harmed. This is emphasised by the fact that neither the characters nor the audience know if Eva/Daisy was actually one girl or not — the Inspector could have put together her story using several different girls that Gerald and the Birlings have mistreated.
- Priestley uses Eva/Daisy to highlight the unfairness of the class system. She has no dialogue in the play and never appears on stage. This emphasises the powerlessness of the working class because, just like in her life, Eva/Daisy has no control over the events that unfold. This is also shown by the way Priestley uses the character of the Inspector to speak for her in her absence.
- Eva/Daisy is used to reveal Gerald and the Birlings' prejudices and prove them wrong. Mr Birling's assumption that she "got herself into trouble" at Milwards is proven wrong when Sheila confesses to getting her sacked. Mr Birling's use of "herself" also emphasises that he believes she is to blame for her actions. By proving that their prejudices are false, Priestley suggests that people should be judged by their actions rather than their class. It also echoes Priestley's socialist view that the class system unfairly victimised the lower class.

Section Three — Context and Themes

Page 24: Britain in 1912 and 1945

1. clear, money, wealthy, poor, charity, restricted, vote, husbands (Other answers are also possible.)
2. The First World War began two years later.
3. E.g."There'll be peace and prosperity and rapid progress everywhere" — The Second World War started in 1939.
4. E.g. No, because the First World War broke out in 1914. This caused a lot of economic hardship in Britain. It's likely that an audience in the mid-1940s would have lived through the depression in the 1930s, which increased unemployment and poverty. They would also have witnessed war breaking out again in 1939.

Page 25: Family Life

1. True, True, True, False
2. E.g. "Arthur, you're not supposed to say such things —" / "Just let me finish, Eric." / "I think it was a mean thing to do."
3. The Inspector's questioning gives Sheila and Eric chance to think for themselves. They are no longer strongly influenced by their parents' views — the authority of the older generation has weakened.
4. E.g. I think the divisions in the Birling family will deepen even further, with Arthur and Sybil on one side, and Eric and Sheila on the other. The younger generation will no longer accept the authority of their parents, which will cause more tension.

Task: Here are some points you may have included:
- Mr Birling fulfils the role of the middle-class father at the beginning of the play. He is the head of the household and asserts his authority, giving "good advice" to the younger generation. He works to support his family and tries to protect the women from distressing events: he doesn't want his daughter to be "dragged into this unpleasant business."
- At the end of the play, he fulfils the same family role. However, it doesn't have the same effect as at the beginning of the play — the Inspector's questioning and Eric and Sheila's refusal to accept his point of view have weakened his authority.
- Sheila is an obedient daughter at the beginning of the play. She fulfils the role expected of a young middle-class woman, listening to the men and taking delight in her engagement.
- Sheila would have been expected to accept the views of her elders, particularly the men, but she stands up to her parents and Gerald at the end of the play when they want to just forget about what happened: "You're pretending everything's just as it was before." This shows that her role has changed.

Pages 26-27: Social Class

1. Working class: Eva/Daisy, e.g. "A good worker too." (Edna is also a possible answer.)
   Middle class: Eric, e.g. "public-school-and-Varsity life" (Sheila, Mr Birling and Mrs Birling are also possible answers.)
   Upper class: Gerald, e.g."your mother — Lady Croft"
2. Sheila used her position as the daughter of a good customer to have Eva/Daisy fired from Milwards.
   Gerald kept Daisy as his mistress with no intention of marrying her. He abandoned her when it suited him.
   Mrs Birling refused to let Eva/Daisy benefit from the charity. She used her influence to turn her away.
3. Mrs Birling is talking about Eva/Daisy in a dismissive, contemptuous way, which suggests that the middle and upper classes were prejudiced against working-class people.
4. Mr Birling looks for ways to improve his position in society.
5. Eric's behaviour is immature and immoral. He drunkenly forces Eva/Daisy to have sex with him and speaks casually about what happened, saying that he was "a bit squiffy". This use of slang suggests that he hasn't grasped the severity of his actions.
6. Priestley wants the audience to feel sorry for Eva Smith, just like Eric does when he calls it a "dam' shame".

Answers

7. The Inspector speaks emotively about Eva/Daisy, describing her as "lonely, half-starved". His language is descriptive, showing that he has thought in detail about the plight of the working class. He recognises the "hopes", "fears" and "suffering" of the "millions" of Eva Smiths that remain.

8. Mr and Mrs Birling assume that working-class people have few morals, but this view is challenged when they learn that Eva/Daisy refused to accept stolen money from Eric. She also acted with dignity when Gerald ended the affair; she was "very gallant".

Task: Here are some points you may have included in Sybil's paragraph:
- Sybil thought Eva/Daisy had low morals and was therefore partly responsible for her condition. This was confirmed (in Sybil's eyes) when she lied about having a husband.
- Sybil thought Eva/Daisy didn't treat her with the respect she deserved and therefore wasn't worthy of charity.
- Sybil believed that her social status allowed her to make decisions — her opinion was the most valid.

Here are some points you may have included in Eva/Daisy's paragraph:
- Eva/Daisy was left in a difficult situation after Eric got her pregnant. She had no family to turn to and the only offer of help she had was stolen money, which she didn't want to accept.
- She lied to Sybil about the baby's father because she thought it might help her case.
- Eva/Daisy used the name 'Mrs Birling' because it really was the first name she'd thought of. She wasn't trying to be disrespectful towards Sybil — it was just bad luck.

Page 28: Young and Old

1. older, traditional, respected, Sheila, Eric (either way around), challenge, younger, Arthur and Sybil (either way around) (Other answers are also possible.)

2. a) That Mr Birling was too harsh on her.
       E.g. "I call it tough luck."
    b) He is dismissive and gets angry.
       E.g. "What does it matter now...?"
    c) That they haven't understood and will carry on as before.
       E.g. "You're ready to go on in the same old way."

3. Eric and Sheila are prepared to face up to hard truths, but Gerald isn't willing to. This shows that change isn't inevitable just because you're young: you have to make a conscious choice and it can be difficult.

Page 29: Men and Women

1. Various answers are possible, e.g.
- Women are obsessed with clothes and shopping.
  E.g. "I left 'em talking about clothes again."
- Women should be protected by men.
  E.g. "I'm trying to settle it sensibly for you."
- Women are vain.
  E.g. "I caught sight of her smiling at the assistant, and I was furious with her.
- Women are jealous.
  "you might be said to have been jealous of her"
- Women are too emotional.
  E.g. "You be careful — or I'll start weeping."

2. Various answers are possible, e.g.
- Sheila interrupts her father, Gerald and Eric.
- Sheila disagrees with the views of her father and Gerald.
- Sheila decides not to marry Gerald, even though it's expected of her.
- Eva/Daisy stands up to Mr Birling, demanding a higher wage.
- Eva/Daisy refuses Eric's stolen money.
- Eva/Daisy refuses to marry Eric.

3. Eric's language becomes more vulgar, for example he refers to prostitutes as "fat old tarts". Mr Birling speaks more openly — he talks about Eric going "to bed with" Eva/Daisy.

4. Mr Birling has lost control over his family. Eric and Sheila no longer accept his views and constantly contradict him. Mr Birling tries to re-establish his dominance by convincing the others that the Inspector's visit was a hoax, but this is ruined when the phone call leaves him *panic-stricken*.

Page 30: Judgement

1. a) E.g. "I went down myself and told them to clear out"
    b) E.g. "If she'd been some miserable plain little creature, I don't suppose I'd have done it."

2. The Inspector is the barrister asking the questions, and the judge giving his verdict at the end. The Birlings are the defendants and are made to confess their wrongdoings.

3. Eric understands that judgement goes beyond whether something is against the law or not. The Inspector has shown that they have committed moral crimes, even if they can't be arrested for them.

4. It gives the characters chance to debate their own responsibility and pass judgement on each other. They show whether they have learned anything.

Task: Here are some points you may have included:
- The Inspector acts as moral critic
  - Questions morality of characters' actions "Well, he inspected us all right"
  - Reveals evidence to audience then leaves, encouraging characters to judge each other.
  - Audience — no real closure at end, have to come to own conclusions about who was to blame.
- The Inspector reveals different ideas about judgement
  - Gerald: they're "not criminals" vs. Eric: "we all helped to kill her"
  - Gerald + older generation judge themselves using law. ("criminals" = legal terminology). Eric and Sheila judge themselves using morals.
  - Reveals generation divide in play. Eric and Sheila = wider, more mature view of social responsibility.
- Inspector passes sentence on Birlings / Gerald
  - "If men will not learn that lesson, then they will be taught it"
  - "men" = society as a whole. Inspector warning that if selfish actions continue, everyone will suffer. Echoes Priestley's socialism: people are responsible for each other.
  - Relevant to audience of 1945: lived through world war, understand what "fire and blood and anguish" was referring to.

Page 31: Learning About Life

1. The Inspector shows how Mrs Birling is blinded by her prejudices.
    Mrs Birling tries to rewrite events to her own advantage.

2. For: Mr Birling has found out a lot about the immoral actions of his family.
    Against: He hasn't learnt that it's wrong to treat lower-class people badly.

3. Act One: e.g. "Oh I wish you hadn't told me."
    Act Two: e.g. "I know I'm to blame — and I'm desperately sorry —"
    Act Three: e.g. "If it didn't end tragically, then that's lucky for us. But it might have done."

4. He teaches them how hard working-class people have to work in order to survive, and that they often have no one to support them.

Exam Practice:
    Your answer should have an introduction, several paragraphs developing different ideas and a conclusion. You may have included some of the following points:
- Sheila is willing to learn from the Inspector. Initially, she is quite selfish and ignorant, for example she admits that she didn't think getting Eva Smith sacked was "anything very terrible". This shows that she didn't grasp the seriousness of her actions. Later, Sheila starts to consider Eva/Daisy's plight and realises they have all done wrong. Her development

Answers

follows the structure of the play: she learns more and more as the play progresses. By Act Three, Sheila thinks of their actions as "crimes and idiocies." She is able to change her views and she encourages her parents to do likewise.

- Mr Birling's arrogance prevents him from learning. He is set in his ways and won't consider other points of view. His arrogance is clear at the beginning of the play when he calls Eric's concerns about Eva Smith's dismissal "Rubbish!" The force of this short, aggressive exclamation shows how convinced he is of his own opinions. This attitude may have been strengthened by his traditional role as head of the family — he would have been unused to having his authority challenged.

- Mrs Birling's views are similarly unshakeable. Like Mr Birling, she doesn't learn because she refuses to see that she is in the wrong. Even when the Inspector is questioning her, she is adamant that she has done nothing she's "ashamed of". Mr and Mrs Birling finish the play as they started it: convinced of the correctness of their views. Priestley thus shows that learning isn't an automatic process — some characters won't ever change.

Page 32: Social Responsibility

1. You should have completed the table as follows:
   (Gerald) — Thinks business is more important than social responsibility. — Refuses to learn about social responsibility.
   Eric — Aware of the consequences of his actions, more sympathetic towards the working class.
   (Sheila) — Only thinks of her own feelings and happiness. — Feels responsible for Eva/Daisy's death, knows they've all done wrong.

2. E.g. "We are responsible for each other"/ "each of you helped to kill her" / "we'll have to share our guilt"

3. She isn't "ashamed" of the way she treated Eva/Daisy, which shows that she doesn't think it was wrong. This suggests that she has no sense of social responsibility — she doesn't care how her actions and attitudes might affect other people.

4. Arthur Birling is an unpleasant character and the audience doesn't like him. This means they are more inclined to question his views and side with the Inspector, Priestley's 'mouthpiece'.

Task: If you agree with the statement, here are some points you may have included:

- Priestley's message is still relevant today because society is not yet equal, so people who are better off should help those who are less privileged. For example, the Inspector's claim that "We don't live alone... We are responsible for each other" applies to modern society, because it remains true that our actions have an effect on other people.

- Priestley suggests that charity could have saved Eva/Daisy if Mrs Birling had been prepared to help her. There are many charities today which aim to help the less fortunate, and Priestley's message could encourage people to volunteer or donate money.

- Being socially responsible is still important today, as society is more global than it was in 1945, when the play was written. People's lives are now more evidently "intertwined" with the lives of others, meaning that people have more power to reduce inequality on an international scale.

If you disagree with the statement, here are some points you may have included:

- Priestley's message is no longer relevant because society is much more equal today than in 1912, when the play was set. Class divisions are not so obvious.

- Healthcare is more widespread today and there are social benefits for people in need, so someone unemployed like Eva/Daisy would be able to get help in our society, instead of having to rely on the generosity of wealthier people like Gerald. She would get free healthcare so she wouldn't need to rely on a charity such as Mrs Birling's when pregnant.

- The "suffering and happiness" of others are not "intertwined with our lives" because there is more of a focus on independence in today's society. People are encouraged to make their own way in life.

Page 33: Skills Focus — Writing About Context

1. a) at the start of the 20th century children were expected to respect their parents' authority. Families had a clear structure, with the father at the top of the hierarchy. / which goes against the social expectation of the time.

   b) At the time the play is set, there was a rigid class system and those in society with the most money had the most power.

2. E.g. In 1912, there were different expectations about how men and women should behave. It would have been unthinkable for an upper- or middle-class woman to behave like Gerald, but he gets away with it because he is a wealthy man with a secure social position.

Page 34: Practice Questions

Each answer should have an introduction, several paragraphs developing different ideas and a conclusion. You may have included some of the following points:

1.
- Birling family life is portrayed as harmonious at the beginning of the play, but cracks emerge once the Inspector begins his questioning. A division develops, with Sheila and Eric on one side, and Mr and Mrs Birling on the other. Sheila and Eric disagree with Mr Birling's treatment of Eva Smith. Sheila calls it "a rotten shame" and Eric describes it as "tough luck". Their emphatic language shows that they are starting to disapprove of the older generation's attitude. The fact that Sheila and Eric disagree with their parents defies the social expectation of the time that the young should automatically respect the authority of their parents.

- The older generation becomes equally disapproving of the behaviour of some members of the younger generation. Mrs Birling is horrified when she finds out about Eric's drinking and his affair with Eva/Daisy. His behaviour encourages the older generation to believe that the young are irresponsible and should respect their elders. This divide remains until the end of Act Three, when Mr and Mrs Birling dismiss Eric and Sheila's concerns.

- Priestley also creates tension using the theme of learning about life. Sheila is frustrated by her parents' refusal to learn from their mistakes, reprimanding Mr Birling for his insistence that the Inspector wasn't really a police officer. She speaks *"flaring up"*, which conveys her anger to the audience. Her use of direct, critical language when she talks about the family "dodging and pretending" contrasts with her father's attitude, as he sees the Inspector's visit as a joke. This shows she has grasped the Inspector's message about the importance of learning from her mistakes while her father has not. Priestley is suggesting to the audience that the older generation find it harder to learn than the younger generation.

2.
- Sheila's behaviour doesn't conform to the role that a middle-class woman was expected to have. Women were supposed to prioritise family life and be obedient to men, but Sheila breaks off her engagement to Gerald, returning his ring. This shows that she is acting independently and starting to think for herself. The audience realises that the Inspector's questioning has encouraged Sheila to break away from expectations. Priestley shows that this is positive because by becoming more independent, Sheila is able to understand the Inspector's message and take responsibility for her actions.

- Priestley also challenges gender roles by having Sheila contradict her father when he tries to defend Gerald's affair. She uses authoritative language, cutting into his dialogue and saying "Don't interfere, please, Father." She speaks politely, using the word "please", but forcefully using an imperative, showing that she is sure of her own views and gaining maturity. Here, Sheila is challenging the stereotype of the obedient middle-class woman. This is a big contrast to the beginning of the play, where she listens respectfully to Mr Birling's speech. Priestley shows that challenging gender roles is positive by portraying Mr Birling as an unpleasant, arrogant character whose views shouldn't be accepted unquestioningly.

- Priestley also uses the character of Eva/Daisy to challenge gender roles throughout the play. Eva/Daisy is presented as an independent and assertive woman. This is shown by her request for higher wages at Mr Birling's factory. She stood up for what she wanted, even though it meant challenging a male superior. Mr Birling's behaviour is condemned by the Inspector, which suggests that he thinks Eva/Daisy's behaviour was morally acceptable. Their conflicting views encourage the audience to think about their own attitudes towards gender inequality.

3. • Mrs Birling belongs to the higher classes, but she acts immorally. When asked if she refused to help Eva/Daisy because of her own prejudice, she simply replies "Yes." This short, matter-of-fact reply has a finality to it which demonstrates how ingrained her self belief is — she doesn't feel any need to justify her uncaring actions. *An Inspector Calls* is set in 1912 when many people thought that the higher classes behaved better than the lower classes. This idea is challenged by Priestley's portrayal of Mrs Birling: her immoral behaviour leads directly to Eva/Daisy's death.

- Mr and Mrs Birling's different reactions to Eric and Gerald's immoral behaviour highlight the hypocrisy of the higher classes. Gerald's affair with Eva/Daisy isn't considered as shocking as Eric's actions because he managed to hide it and end it without consequences. Priestley therefore reveals the hypocrisy of the family: they judge the working class as 'immoral', but they will tolerate immoral behaviour from members of their own social class, as long as it doesn't create a scandal. This hypocrisy encourages the audience to scorn Mr and Mrs Birling's attitude towards the lower classes.

- Eva/Daisy, who belongs to the working class, is arguably the most moral character in the play. For example, she refuses to accept Eric's stolen money. This challenges the belief that the working class was less moral than the higher classes which Mr Birling presents when he assumes that Eva/Daisy "got herself into trouble" at Milwards. The form of *An Inspector Calls* is significant here: it has some of the features of a morality play. Priestley encourages the audience to judge the characters' prejudices, but also to question their own morality.

4. • The Inspector's questioning shows how the Birlings and Gerald all contributed to Eva/Daisy's death through their socially irresponsible behaviour. He describes their actions as a "chain of events" which demonstrates that a person's actions can have an effect on others. This reflects Priestley's socialist view that everyone is responsible for everyone else. In this way, the Inspector is Priestley's 'mouthpiece', and he shows the audience how important it is to think about the consequences before you act.

- The fact that the Inspector challenges middle- and upper-class characters about their immoral behaviour suggests that everyone has a social responsibility towards others. He questions Mrs Birling's honesty — "You're not telling me the truth" — even though she is his social superior. His blunt, forceful language directly contradicts her; it is as though he is scolding a child. This puts the Inspector in a position of authority and suggests to the audience that a person's social responsibility shouldn't be influenced by their class status. This is highlighted by the fact that Priestley presents the Inspector as classless — he is the only person in the play whose character isn't defined by their social status.

- *An Inspector Calls* takes a similar form to a morality play, as Priestley uses the Inspector to convey a moral lesson to the audience. In his final speech, the Inspector warns that "We are responsible for each other" and that ignoring this responsibility will lead to "fire and blood and anguish". He is no longer just referring to the Birling family, but to society as a whole. His suggestion that a lack of responsibility will have

disastrous consequences makes the audience consider how responsible they are for their own actions.

5. • In the early 20th century, when the play is set, there was a clearly defined class system. Class is a key theme throughout the play, and Priestley shows that this rigid social structure had a negative effect on members of the working class. Priestley uses the play's structure to encourage the audience to think about the injustice of this. The revelations about the characters' involvement with Eva/Daisy gradually build up, supporting the idea that the class system allows the working class to be exploited. By the time the play reaches its climax and another inspector is on his way, the audience is convinced that the Birlings and Gerald are guilty, and they are ready to reconsider their own class prejudices.

- Setting the play in 1912 also gave Priestley the opportunity to explore the injustice of the clearly defined gender roles of that period. For example, Mrs Birling tells Sheila that she should expect her husband to be busy with his "important work", implying that she shouldn't question Gerald's actions. Priestley later reveals that Sheila's suspicions were correct, which undermines the idea that women shouldn't question their husbands. Gender roles had been broken down to some extent by the time Priestley was writing, but Priestley reminds the audience of the injustice of gender inequality.

- Setting the play in 1912 gave Priestley the benefit of hindsight. Mr Birling is shown to be ignorant by making predictions that won't come true, such as "And I say there isn't a chance of war." His use of the first person pronoun "I" when discussing such an important topic illustrates how greatly he values his own opinion. This dramatic irony would be clear to an audience watching in the 1940s or later, who would know just how mistaken he is. This means that Arthur's judgement on other matters, such as social responsibility, is called into question. Priestley uses the Inspector to convey his own views, so he wants the audience to share the Inspector's beliefs, not Arthur's.

Section Four — The Writer's Techniques

Page 35: 'An Inspector Calls' on the Stage

1. A claustrophobic / intense / oppressive atmosphere.
2. a) "brighter and harder"
   b) E.g. To make the atmosphere less cosy. The light is like a spotlight, making it easier for the characters to be examined.
3. E.g. The Birling house has good quality furniture / there are dessert plates and champagne glasses.
4. To make the Inspector stand out from the others and show that he doesn't have the same class background or values.
5. You should have ticked all of the statements.
Task: E.g. A small tropical island. This would be suitable because you can't easily escape from a desert island, so it would feel claustrophobic. It's also a place that's known to be comfortable and relaxing, so the Inspector's visit would be seen as an unwelcome intrusion.

Pages 36-37: Dramatic Techniques

1. Gerald confesses to Sheila, but he wants to keep it secret from the Inspector. Act One then ends and the audience is left wondering if the Inspector will make him confess.
2. After Gerald's initial confession to Sheila, Priestley changes the focus of the action in Act Two to other characters. The audience is forced to wait for his explanation.
3. It makes the existence of multiple Evas/Daisies seem like a strong possibility.
4. It means that the audience is gradually fed information about what happened to Eva/Daisy. They begin to wonder who will be questioned next and how they are involved.
5. a) E.g. It suggests to the audience that Sheila is the customer who complained and got Eva/Daisy sacked from Milwards.
   b) E.g. It creates tension because he is the only character on stage who doesn't know what Mrs Birling has done.

Answers

6.   door, audience, tone, dialogue, tension
7.   E.g. He decides who he is going to question and when. / He slowly reveals what he knows about Eva/Daisy.
8.   celebratory: when the Birlings are toasting the engagement
sad: when Gerald leaves after admitting the affair
threatening: when the Inspector delivers his final speech
9. a) Because the plot revolves around finding out who is responsible for Eva/Daisy's death.
   b) Because the play is designed to teach the audience a lesson.

Exam Practice:
    Your answer should have an introduction, several paragraphs developing different ideas and a conclusion. You may have included some of the following points:
- Priestley uses the character of the Inspector to build excitement in the plot. His method of examining "one line of inquiry at a time" allows the pace of the action to gradually build, as each confession seems more shocking than the last. This develops excitement among the audience as the play progresses and they want to find out more. It also makes the audience feel as though the plot is heading towards an inevitable crisis.
- Priestley also uses the timing of entrances and exits to build excitement in the plot. In Act Two, just as Sheila begins to question the true nature of the Inspector, Mrs Birling re-enters the dining room. Her "*brisk*" manner is "*quite out of key*" with what has just happened, and her re-appearance moves the action away from Sheila. The audience is left to imagine why Sheila was staring at the Inspector "*wonderingly and dubiously*", which builds intrigue as the other characters don't initially share her suspicions. Mrs Birling's entrance in Act Two also enables Priestley to increase suspense because Gerald's full confession is delayed further.
- The play is set in a single room. This creates excitement as Priestley provides no relief from the growing tension in the house. Priestley uses language related to heat to highlight the intense atmosphere that develops. In Act Two, Mr Birling is described as "*hot, bothered*" and by Act Three he speaks "*explosively*". Furthermore, it's only when Gerald leaves that he is able to "cool off". This suggests that the atmosphere in the house becomes close and claustrophobic. This atmosphere also helps to unsettle Gerald and the Birlings, which makes it easier for the Inspector to uncover the truth about their actions and force them to accept responsibility.

Page 38: Priestley's Use of Language

1.   E.g. "chaps" / "Jingo"
2.   It makes the characters seem more realistic. This helps the Inspector's message feel more relevant to the audience.
3.   He has the same accent as 'common' people, which suggests he doesn't come from a wealthy background.
4. a) She expects to be respected and not challenged.
   b) The Inspector is rude and doesn't respect Mrs Birling or recognise her authority. He isn't afraid to challenge her.
5.   Sheila's language is childish at the beginning of the play, but as her attitude becomes more mature, her language grows more sophisticated. She expresses herself plainly and speaks with more passion and honesty.

Page 39: Language Techniques

1.   E.g. "we're in for a time of steadily increasing prosperity."
The audience knows that Britain went to war shortly after and suffered a depression, so this makes Mr Birling seem foolish.
2.   It suggests that they don't want to confront unpleasant facts about real life and would rather just avoid them.
3.   Imagery (effect): E.g. The words "fire", "blood" and "anguish" create an ominous picture of the future, especially as they're similar to the words used in the Bible to describe the end of the world.
First-person plural (example): E.g. "We are members of one body."
First-person plural (effect): E.g. It makes the audience feel as

though the Inspector is including them in his speech. This helps Priestley put across the play's message.
Repetition (example): "millions and millions and millions of Eva Smiths"
Repetition (effect): This stresses that Eva/Daisy's story isn't an exception and that social injustice exists on a large scale.
4.   To shock the other characters and make them feel guilty about Eva/Daisy's death.

Page 40: Skills Focus — Staging and Dramatic Techniques

1. a) E.g. Mr Birling and Gerald "*both laugh*" just before Eric enters. This creates the impression of unity between them — Eric is not included.
   b) E.g. Eric's speech is inconsistent and broken: first he speaks "*eagerly*", then he is "*confused*" — he seems to be uncomfortable. Also, he "*checks himself*" — he realises he has said too much.
2.   E.g. They suggest that Mrs Birling is unpleasant. She doesn't want to cooperate and seems rude when she speaks to the Inspector.
3.   E.g. "*coolly*", "*calmly*", "*massively*"
The stage directions show that the Inspector is in command of himself and of the situation, unlike the Birlings who often become emotional. He is controlling events.

Page 41: Practice Questions

    Each answer should have an introduction, several paragraphs developing different ideas and a conclusion. You may have included some of the following points:
1.
- Priestley's decision to set the play in the Birlings' dining room creates a divide between the private lives of the Birlings and the 'real' world outside. The Inspector is shown to be an unwelcome outsider in the house, who turns their "family celebration" into a "nasty mess". The word "nasty" suggests that there is something sinister and unpleasant about the situation the Birlings are now in; the Inspector's intrusion into their home introduces uncomfortable external realities that Gerald and the Birlings cannot avoid. These realities are used to draw out family tensions that already exist below the surface, for example Eric's drinking problem.
- Priestley uses the setting to force the Birlings to confront their actions. The play is set inside the Birlings' house, which prevents them from easily avoiding the Inspector's questions. When Eric wants to escape by going to bed, the Inspector states that he might just have to "turn out again soon." The fact that all the characters are made to confess in the same setting also encourages the audience to compare their different attitudes towards accepting responsibility for Eva/Daisy's death.
- The quiet and confined atmosphere of the setting allows small noises in the house take on a greater significance, which allows Priestley to create tension. The "*sharp ring*" of the doorbell announces the Inspector's arrival, and when the phone rings at the end of the play it too "*rings sharply*". The word 'sharp' shows that these noises are shrill, which suggests that they have an unsettling effect on the household. The fact that the ringing of the phone is followed by a "*moment's compete silence*" reveals how intrusive this unsettling effect is — every character on stage is brought to a standstill.
2.
- *An Inspector Calls* has elements of a murder mystery story, which creates tension and suspense. The Inspector's treatment of Gerald and the Birlings as suspects creates tension in the play because they're forced to adopt a defensive attitude towards the Inspector. Gerald tells him "we're respectable citizens and not criminals". This suggests to the audience that Gerald believes they're being treated unfairly, which creates a sense of conflict. The Inspector's extensive knowledge and method of interviewing one character at a time adds to the suspense, as each confession feeds the audience information about Eva/Daisy bit by bit.

Answers

- Priestley uses the staging of the play to create tension. Before the Inspector arrives, the lighting is "*pink and intimate*", which makes the audience feel relaxed. When the Inspector arrives, the lighting becomes "*brighter and harder*". The word "*harder*" contrasts with the comfort implied by the initial pink lighting, which makes the mood more serious. This change in atmosphere makes the scene more tense. The brighter stage also gives the audience the impression that Gerald and the Birlings are being examined under a spotlight, and makes the audience wonder what the Inspector will discover.
- Priestley structures entrances and exits in the play to increase tension. Eric leaves the house before Mrs Birling's confession, which allows her to condemn him unknowingly. Sheila is the first to realise Mrs Birling's mistake and she attempts to stop her mother: "Mother — don't you see?" This creates suspense because the audience becomes aware of the Inspector's trap just as Mrs Birling is falling into it. Furthermore, the act ends just as Eric returns. This means the action is paused just before Eric is confronted by his family and the Inspector. The audience is left anticipating the conflict that will occur at the start of the next act.

3.
- The difference in atmosphere before and after the Inspector's visit shows the audience the impact the Inspector has had on the characters' attitudes. At the start of the play, the atmosphere is light-hearted. After the Inspector leaves, even when he is thought to be a hoax, the characters can't recover their initial mood of celebration. This is highlighted by the fact that Sheila refuses to reinstate her engagement with Gerald, suggesting that she can't return to the person she was at the start of the play. This reveals to the audience that the Inspector's investigation has permanently altered relations within the Birling family.
- Priestley destroys the celebratory mood at the start of the play to show that the happiness in the Birlings' private lives is a pretence. As the Inspector questions them, the atmosphere changes from one where they are all "*pleased with themselves*" to one of conflict. For example, when Eric disagrees with Arthur in Act One, Arthur snaps at his son in front of Gerald and the Inspector, saying it's time he "learnt to face a few responsibilities." The fact that this conflict arises so early in the play suggests that there was pre-existing tension in their relationship. By showing that the Birling's happy family life is an act, Priestley encourages the audience to question the authenticity of other aspects of their life, like their respectability as a middle-class family.
- The Inspector creates a threatening atmosphere by issuing ominous warnings in the play. The Inspector's prediction that their attitudes could result in "fire" and "blood" and "anguish" uses powerful and threatening imagery and references language used in the Bible to describe the end of the world. This reinforces Priestley's message that if the characters, and by extension the higher classes in society, don't change their attitudes, then the consequences will be disastrous. The final phone call recreates this threatening atmosphere, leaving Mr Birling "*panic-stricken*". This ensures the play ends on a cautionary note to emphasise Priestley's warning about the attitudes of the higher classes towards social responsibility.

4.
- Priestley's decision to have the events in the play unfold over the course of one evening allows him to focus on developing conflicts between the characters. Changes in their relationships are felt more keenly by the audience because they are witnessing the changes in real time. For example, the audience anticipates the open conflict between Mrs Birling and Eric at the start of Act Three because they have just witnessed Mrs Birling realising that he got Eva/Daisy pregnant. This draws the audience into their conflict and allows Priestley to emphasise Mrs Birling's hypocritical views.
- Priestley uses the costumes of the Inspector and Mr Birling to present a conflict over different attitudes towards class. The Inspector's "*plain darkish suit*" sets him apart from Mr Birling's "*evening dress*". Mr Birling's costume clearly identifies him

as middle class, while the Inspector's outfit is nondescript, implying that he doesn't belong to a specific class. Their contrasting costumes highlight their attitudes towards social class: Mr Birling conforms to the traditional class system of the period, while the Inspector rejects it. The fact that their different costumes establish them as opposites at the start of the play is also important for conflict in the play as a whole, as it places tension at the centre of their relationship.
- Conflict between different characters is shown by the language they use. The Inspector speaks directly, describing Eva/Daisy as lying on a slab with "a burnt-out inside". His description uses sharp 't' and 'd' sounds, which show the harsh reality of Eva/Daisy's suicide. In contrast, Mrs Birling uses euphemisms to describe Eva/Daisy, referring to her as "a girl in her position." This shows their different attitudes towards society — Mrs Birling believes she can ignore unpleasant realities, but the Inspector thinks everyone should face up to them. The eager way Mrs Birling readily accepts that the Inspector was a hoax in Act Three highlights that this belief remains unchanged at the end of the play.

5.
- Priestley builds up trust between the audience and the Inspector. The way the Inspector cuts across other characters "*massively*" and reprimands them — "each of you helped to kill her" — gives his character authority and a moral superiority. This trust between the audience and the Inspector is important for the play's moral: it makes the audience more likely to accept the message Priestley delivers in the Inspector's final speech. The fact that characters who disagree with him (like Mr and Mrs Birling) are portrayed negatively also encourages the audience to take on the Inspector's message.
- The audience is made to feel sympathy for Eva/Daisy. She is presented as a victim in the play, whose death was a result of the other characters' selfishness and ignorance. The Inspector reveals that she died in "agony", in need of "money", "advice", "sympathy" and "friendliness". Emotive language like "agony" encourages the audience to view her suicide as a tragedy. The way the Inspector provides a long list of the things Eva/Daisy died in need of also highlights her deprivation and desperation which is a result of the other characters' actions. By using the Inspector in this way, Priestley encourages the audience to share in his views about social responsibility.
- Priestley deliberately withholds information in the play, making the audience feel tense and excited because they want to find out the truth. They are never shown the photograph of Eva/Daisy and, like Gerald and the Birlings, they are kept guessing about the Inspector's real identity. This mystery creates suspense, which helps to keep the audience's attention. It also makes the audience reliant on the Inspector for information. This gives the play important elements of a 'murder mystery' story, which emphasises the theme of judgement.

Section Five — Exam Buster

Page 42: Understanding the Question

1. b) <u>What</u> is the <u>significance</u> of <u>Mr Birling</u> in *An Inspector Calls*?
   c) <u>Explain</u> <u>how</u> the theme of <u>family life</u> is <u>explored</u> in *An Inspector Calls*.
   d) <u>How</u> is <u>staging</u> used to create <u>suspense</u> in *An Inspector Calls*?
   e) <u>Explain</u> the <u>importance</u> of <u>gender roles</u> in the play.
   f) <u>How</u> is the character of <u>Mrs Birling</u> <u>presented</u> in *An Inspector Calls*?
   g) <u>Explain</u> <u>why</u> <u>Eric</u> <u>changes</u> in the play.
2. a - 5, b - 1, c - 4, d - 2, e - 3

Page 43: Making a Rough Plan

1. E.g. Mr Birling wants to improve his social status. / Mrs Birling is prejudiced against the working class. / Gerald uses Eva/Daisy for his own amusement. / Sheila exploits her power over Eva/Daisy.

Answers

2. Pick your three most important points and put them in a sensible order. Write down a quote or an example from the play that backs them up.

Page 44: Making Links

1. Arthur and Sybil have traditional views. E.g. Mrs Birling tells Sheila not to tease Gerald.
   Sheila challenges her parents' authority. E.g. Sheila contradicts her father by saying "it was anything but a joke."
   Gerald is young but shares the views of the older generation. E.g. He thinks everything is fine again at the end of the play.
2. E.g. If one of your points was 'Mrs Birling is prejudiced against the working class' and your evidence was that Mrs Birling used her influence to have Eva/Daisy's request for help refused, you could link it to the fact that Mrs Birling refers to Eva/Daisy as "a girl of that sort."

Page 45: Structuring Your Answer

1. Point: Gerald shares many of Arthur Birling's views, particularly about business.
   Example: Arthur "couldn't have done anything else" with regards to sacking Eva Smith.
   Explain: Like Arthur, he also lacks social responsibility and thinks that it's acceptable to prioritise profit over his employees' wellbeing.
   Develop: The similarity between Gerald and Mr Birling is also shown at the end of the play, when they are both happy to believe that it was all a hoax.
2. a) Eric is "ashamed" of his parents.
   b) Mr Birling is worried that there could be a "public scandal".
3. E.g. Point: Mrs Birling is prejudiced against the working class.
   Example: She refers to Eva/Daisy as "a girl of that sort."
   Explain: This shows that she assumes working-class people have lower morals than middle-class or upper-class people.
   Develop: This is also shown when she uses her influence to have Eva/Daisy's request for help refused.

Page 46: Introductions and Conclusions

1. Intro b) is better, e.g. Intro a) makes points which aren't relevant to the question, such as Arthur Birling not getting on with Eric.
2. E.g. The first sentence should be made relevant to the question by mentioning social responsibility. No new points should be introduced — the conclusion should give a summary of the points already made in the essay.
Task: Your introduction and conclusion should both give a clear answer to the question. The introduction should include your main points, but no evidence. Your conclusion should summarise your argument and not include new points.

Page 47: Writing about Context

1. a - 2, b - 1, c - 3
2. Contextual information: This reflects Priestley's belief that power and wealth were shared out unequally in society in the early 20th century.
   You could have included context as the Explain or Develop part of the paragraph. The context you wrote about should be relevant to your Point and linked to the Example.

Page 48: Linking Ideas and Paragraphs

1. E.g. Sheila challenges her parents' views. For example, when Mr and Mrs Birling are relieved that there is no Inspector Goole on the police force, Sheila says sarcastically that they are "all nice people" again. This shows that she knows that they have still made terrible mistakes and can't just move on. She stands up to her parents because she wants them to realise this.
2. You should have used the P.E.E.D. structure and included connecting words and phrases such as 'therefore' or 'for example' to link your ideas.
3. E.g. Priestley also explores the theme of social class by... This idea is developed further when...

Page 49: Marking Answer Extracts

1. 4-5: The answer gives a thoughtful personal response to the text and shows an understanding of contextual factors. However, the analysis of Priestley's language isn't detailed enough for it to be a 6-7 answer. There are some spelling and punctuation errors, and the range of vocabulary and sentence structures is limited.

Page 50: Marking Answer Extracts

1. a) 8-9: E.g. "Eric's inappropriate laughter and loud speech... Birling family life." — an insightful and critical personal response
   "Priestley's presentation of Eric... benefitted those at the top" — detailed exploration of the relationship between the text and its context
   b) 6-7: E.g. "Priestley achieves this... drunkenly forced himself on Eva/Daisy." — integrated, well-chosen examples
   "The strength of Eric's feelings... makes him seem vulnerable." — thorough exploration of how the writer uses language

Pages 51-52: Marking a Whole Answer

1. 8-9: E.g. The answer examines several different aspects of context in detail, including gender roles, class and Priestley's views on these. There is close and perceptive analysis of language, for example the examination of Priestley's use of imagery in the third paragraph.

Page 53: Skills Focus — Writing Well

1. The audience witnesses the gradual breakdown of the Briling [Birling] family structure. After the Inspector leaves in Act Three, Shiela [Sheila] and Eric challenge there [their] parents. Mrs Birling trys [tries] to show that she is in charge, telling sheila [Sheila] not to be "childish", but Sheila replies, "it's you to [two] who are being childish. [childish".] Sheila disagrees with how her parent's [parents] are behaving.
2. You could have rewritten the sentences as follows:
   a) The Inspector appears mysterious because his origins are unknown.
   b) Mrs Birling is a highly unpleasant character who behaves heartlessly towards Eva/Daisy.
   c) The Birlings argue frequently.
   d) Priestley uses staging effectively to create tension in the play.

Page 54: Practice Questions

Each answer should have an introduction, several paragraphs developing different ideas and a conclusion. You may have included some of the following points:

1. • The play takes the form of a mystery story — both the audience and the characters have to piece together events before a final revelation. The Inspector deals with "one line of inquiry at a time". This means that the audience is left guessing from the beginning, but won't find out what all of the characters did until Act Three. This sense of mystery creates a feeling of tension and suspense for the audience.
   • Cliffhangers also add to the sense of mystery by leaving events unresolved at the end of each act. This is particularly apparent at the end of Act Three, when Priestley creates a cliffhanger by having the curtain fall just after Mr Birling tells the others that another Inspector is "on his way" — the audience therefore has no idea what will happen next. This allows the audience to interpret the play's events and imagine subsequent occurrences in their own way.
   • The Inspector himself is a very mysterious character. His origins are unknown and his use of language suggests that he is not like a normal police inspector. For example, his final speech has a preachy tone. He employs rhetorical devices such as using three consecutive short statements starting with "We..." to emphasise the fact that his message is for all humanity. This shows that he is giving a moral lesson,

Answers

whereas a normal police officer would stick to facts. His sudden disappearance towards the end of the action adds to the sense of mystery surrounding him.

2. • Priestley uses the character of Eva/Daisy to explore the idea that prejudice is often unfounded. Mrs Birling can't believe that a working-class girl would have refused stolen money, because she imagines that working-class people have lower standards of morality. Priestley uses the play's structure to present a dramatic challenge to this prejudice: it is suddenly revealed that Eric is the immoral one. Priestley simultaneously forces the audience to examine the accuracy of their own prejudices.

   • The character of Eva/Daisy also has the function of demonstrating how deeply ingrained prejudice can be. Priestley achieves this through showing the other characters' responses to her tragic demise. Although Mrs Birling knows that Eva/Daisy died a "horrible death", she states that the girl "had only herself to blame". This dismissive attitude shows that her prejudices are more powerful than any feelings of human sympathy she might have. Even when she finds out that Eva/Daisy wasn't to blame, she puts the responsibility on the father instead, assuming that he is working-class and therefore immoral.

   • By having the characters on stage gradually piece together the chain of events that led to Eva/Daisy's death, Priestley also shows how small acts of prejudice can have huge consequences. For example, in isolation, Mrs Birling's refusal to help someone she disapproved of might not appear very significant. As part of a series of misfortunes, however, it was catastrophic, destroying Eva/Daisy's last hope. This reinforces Priestley's message — we are all linked, so we are responsible for actions which affect other people.

3. • At the start of An Inspector Calls, Arthur Birling behaves in an authoritative, confident manner towards his family. He clearly wants to be seen as the strong head of the household and makes bold statements about politics, talking about "silly little war scares". This language plays down the threat of war, which creates an impression of extreme confidence. This conforms to the social expectation of the time that the husband and father should be the dominant member of the family. However, Arthur is shown to be insecure around Gerald through his use of hesitant, disrupted language when he speaks about Gerald's mother's concerns, saying "your mother — Lady Croft — while she doesn't object... — feels you might have done better". Arthur is insecure because his family is socially inferior to Gerald's.

   • Arthur's position is undermined through his conflict with Eric, who clearly doesn't respect him. Their relationship deteriorates as the play progresses and by Act Three Eric is openly challenging Arthur, "laughing" at Arthur's concern about his knighthood and saying he's "ashamed" of his parents' actions. This shows that Arthur has not created the position he desires for himself. At the start of the 20th century, sons were expected to respect their fathers' authority, but Eric defies this role.

   • It appears that Arthur's position has been reinstated towards the end of Act Three when he is convinced that the Inspector's visit was a hoax. He speaks "triumphantly" and his confidence is displayed through his use of short, decisive phrases: "Don't talk rubbish. Of course it is." However, Priestley plays a structural trick, quickly reversing Arthur's gains with the final phone call which leaves him "panic-stricken". Arthur has no time to reestablish his position before the curtain falls. The impression the audience is left with is one of uncertainty and weakness.

4. • Gerald represents the privileged higher classes. Through him, Priestley shows that life is easier with the advantages of a good social position and wealth. For example, Gerald has a much smaller risk of facing consequences for his actions than Eric. Unlike Eric, who had to rely on stealing from his father, Gerald was able to give Eva/Daisy a "parting gift of enough money" for the next few months. This meant that he

could leave her without creating a messy situation. Even the Inspector can't find much to criticise Gerald for, conceding that he made Eva/Daisy "happy for a time"

   • The fact that Mr Birling is so keen to impress Gerald, a much younger man, shows that a high social class was something that people aspired to at the time An Inspector Calls is set. Mr Birling wants to win over Gerald with talk of a "knighthood", which suggests that he wants to be seen as belonging to Gerald's world. This also makes Mr Birling's anxiousness about his social position clear to the audience.

   • Gerald is also used to explore ideas about gender roles. Although Sheila challenges Gerald and breaks off their engagement, he doesn't take her seriously, and by the end of Act Three he expects that Sheila will want to marry him again, asking "What about this ring?" This language is casual and confident, suggesting that he thinks he is in control of the situation. This shows that his traditional family views are deeply ingrained — he doesn't think a woman can be serious about independence, and so assumes that Sheila will still want to marry him. His reference to the "ring" and not to marriage makes the audience think back to Act One where all Sheila cared about was marriage and clothes. This reference emphasises that Gerald doesn't understand how or why Sheila has changed.

5. • From Mr Birling's treatment of Eva/Daisy, the audience can learn about the importance of social responsibility in business. He expresses the need to "come down sharply" on those who rebel, and this attitude led to him sacking Eva Smith. As the Inspector suggests, this sparked a "chain of events" which ultimately led to the girl's suicide. If Mr Birling had given her a second chance instead, Eva/Daisy's life could have been saved. This shows the audience how important it is that businessmen take responsibility for their employees' wellbeing and don't merely focus on cutting costs.

   • Sheila's part in the story teaches the audience about the importance of social responsibility in everyday life. Sheila had Eva/Daisy sacked from her job at Milwards out of vanity, which left Eva/Daisy close to poverty, forcing her to become a prostitute. Priestley uses Sheila to demonstrate how a seemingly insignificant action can have disastrous consequences for someone else. Priestley uses the structure of the play to reinforce this idea. By revealing each character's involvement in turn and showing that the unfortunate results were preventable, the audience is encouraged to think about how their own actions could have unforeseen consequences. This emphasises the need for socially responsible behaviour in daily life.

   • An Inspector Calls has a form similar to a morality play with a clear moral message at the end about the importance of social responsibilty. However, Priestley uses stage directions to show that becoming socially responsible is a difficult process. Mr Birling is "amused" and Gerald is "smiling" towards the end of Act Three, while Sheila speaks "passionately" — clearly, she is still distressed. The effect of this is that the audience sees that accepting responsibility for your actions towards others is the difficult path; it's a painful process. However, Sheila and Eric's refusal to return to the way they were before the revelations suggests that once a person has made the change, they do not want to, or are unable to, become ignorant again.

The Characters from 'An Inspector Calls'

Phew! After tackling all those questions, I reckon you deserve a bit of a break. So grab a cup of tea and your favourite kind of biscuit, make yourself comfortable and enjoy *An Inspector Calls — The Cartoon...*

Arthur Birling

The Inspector

Sybil Birling

Gerald Croft

Eva Smith / Daisy Renton

Eric Birling

Edna

Sheila Birling

J. B. Priestley's 'An Inspector Calls'